CLEAN GREEN EATS

CLEAN

HARPER WAVE

An Imprint of HarperCollins*Publishers*

GREEN EATS

100+ Clean-Eating Recipes to Improve Your Whole Life

Candice Kumai

HarperCollins books may be purchased for educational, business, or sales promotional use. For information, please e-mail the Special Markets Department at SPsales@harpercollins.com.

FIRST EDITION

Designed by Leah Carlson-Stanisic

Photography by Evi Abeler

Library of Congress Cataloging-in-Publication Data

Kumai, Candice.
    Clean green eats : 100+ clean-eating recipes to improve your whole life / Candice Kumai.—First edition.
        pages   cm
    ISBN 978-0-06-238873-5
    1. Cooking (Vegetables) 2. Vegetable juices. 3. Nutrition. 4. Detoxification (Health) 5. Self-care, Health. I. Title.
        TX801.K86   2015
        641.5'636—dc23   2015009848

    16 17 18 19   OV/RRD   10 9 8 7 6 5

For Dad,

Dad, for your incredible heart, your unmeasurable integrity, for your wisdom & kindness. This book is for you. Thank you for being such a rock for us. Your years of hard work & how you led by example will help to make this world a better place.

For your love, I am grateful

Dad, Poland, 1954.

CONTENTS

PREFACE

WHOLE FOODS MAKE YOU FEEL GOOD,
AND, WHEN YOU FEEL GOOD, YOUR WHOLE
LIFE STARTS TO IMPROVE.

I grew up eating wholesome, fresh Californian produce, and learned to cook super-nutritious Japanese cuisine, compliments of my Japanese mom. Today, my primary job as a chef, food writer, and health journalist is to share what I know and love about food, culture, heritage, sustainability, and health. I love food, real and clean food, from the heart. And after almost two decades of working in the food and health industry—learning new culinary techniques, cooking in restaurants, tasting food prepared by accomplished chefs, developing fresh and healthy recipes for magazines and books, traveling the globe in search of new cultures and ingredients, and working with organic farmers across the country—I've found that I have come full circle: back to simplicity, back to cooking real food. Trends are nice and all, but real food is here to stay, forever.

I've seen, touched, sampled, and tested enough to know what tastes amazing, looks gorgeous, and nurtures your body back to health, and it all starts with clean, green food. Green foods nurture your body and mind with vitamins and nutrients like calcium, fiber, potassium, and magnesium. By eating more real, whole foods, you will help to protect your body against disease, reduce inflammation, and simultaneously, you'll look and feel absolutely radiant—and you don't have to have the same boring salad every day to reap these rewards. Who doesn't want a sweet potato burger with sliced avocado or a hot bowl of kale fried rice? This isn't about eating "health" food: it's about eating real food, prepared deliciously.

I have to give *all* of the credit for the way I eat to my beautiful mother. It took me a bit of time to realize, but through all of her scolding, she was always right. Fresh fruits and vegetables are the best options to nurture your body. Adding fresh fruits and green brassicas (that's fancy talk for veggies) into your diet will make you glow inside and out. Once you start cooking

Beautiful women don't diet, beautiful women learn to cook. Pass it on.

more often, and adding more greens to your diet, you will never look back. In fact, you will start to *crave more greens*. That chemical-laden processed junk food you used to crave won't even taste good.

There is no place for dieting in my life anymore. And there's no place for it in your life anymore. Let's get back to our mothers' way of eating. When you eat real food, you never have to count calories, worry about fat grams, stress over portion sizes—food should *not* be about guilt or anxiety. The experience of cooking and eating food should be about *pleasure*. Whole foods make you feel good, and, when you feel good, your whole life starts to improve. It's time to stop worrying about food and start savoring it.

Here's the thing: you're already beautiful, inside and out. But how do you *feel*? Do you feel energetic, positive, productive, and light . . . or do you find that you are often fatigued, quick to get sick, headachy, bloated, grumpy, and overall not your best self? Food can change all of that (and help you zip up your favorite jeans, total bonus!). No matter how old you are, good health habits matter, and the sooner you start caring for your body, the larger the rewards. My beautiful Japanese mother has always drunk green tea and eaten fresh fruit and greens daily—and she is healthy and radiant in her sixties. And my dad—who has benefited from my mother's cooking for all of these years—still rides his bike 10 miles a day.

My point is, the decisions we make every day matter—they are cumulative. The best prescription I know for a long, happy, and beautiful life is this: Educate yourself about where your food comes from, grocery shop often, cook most days, exercise, sleep, and enjoy the meals you prepare with the people you love. I hope this book will become your best friend to nurturing yourself back to health and happiness.

CLEAN GREEN EATS

1

HOW TO EAT . . .
AGAIN

THE DOCTOR OF THE FUTURE WILL GIVE NO MEDICINE, BUT WILL
INTEREST HIS PATIENTS IN THE CARE OF THE HUMAN FRAME, IN
DIET, AND IN THE CAUSE AND PREVENTION OF DISEASE.
—*Thomas Edison*

CLEAN EATING: A lifestyle that involves consuming real food in or as close to its most natural state as possible. Eating to nourish and cleanse the body and mind. Educating yourself on where food comes from. Purchasing or growing foods that are nutritious, unprocessed, and sustainable. Being more mindful of your overall health and the environment in which you live. Clean Eating is a choice and a way of life.

Maybe you're someone who doesn't like to cook. I hear you—lots of people tell me they want to eat more healthfully, but they don't like spending time in the kitchen. Well, honey, let me tell you something: Cooking can be fun, cooking can be graceful, cooking can make you feel good, cooking can be the best gift you give yourself every day. It is your greatest resource to finding true health—and delicious food.

More Reasons to Eat Clean and Green

Okay, so you know that eating clean is good for your body. That should be enough to make you turn the pages and start cooking. But if you need more convincing, consider this: Eating clean and cooking green is your new beauty cream. Forget all of the oils and potions, you green beauty queen. Here are three more reasons to eat clean:

1. GREEN IS YOUR BEAUTY CREAM

Beauty is an inside job. Greens are packed with beauty benefits like antioxidants and vitamin C. Antioxidants are also nature's sunblock/beauty serum! They help to prevent free radical damage to your beautiful skin, which may also help to prevent wrinkles. The vitamin C in greens is essential for the formation of collagen. Collagen keeps your hair, skin, and nails strong and even helps keep your body flexible. Yoga, anyone?

Greens are naturally packed with massively powerful antioxidants (vitamin E, folic acid, lycopene, and alpha- and beta-carotene, and more). Antioxidants are substances that protect the body from damage caused by harmful molecules called free radicals. Studies consistently suggest that people whose diets are rich in antioxidant-rich fruits and vegetables may have a lower risk of developing certain types of cancers. So eating more greens helps you look like a beauty queen *and* fight free radicals at the same time . . . smart and stunning, you are!

2. A FLAT TUMMY IS A GREEN TUMMY

Greens are low in carbohydrates, and the carbs they do contain are packed in layers of fiber, which make them very slow to digest. Eating a high-fiber diet keeps your digestive tract happy and helps you lose weight. Why?

Because fiber- and water-packed veggies fill you up quickly and help you stay fuller, longer. And all of that fiber and water helps to prevent bloating, keeping your tummy happy—not to mention, flat. More greens = no more muffin top.

3. GREENS ARE THE FOUNTAIN OF YOUTH

Dark leafy greens, calorie for calorie, are the most concentrated source of nutrition of any food out there. Leafy greens are a rich source of minerals (including iron, calcium, potassium, and magnesium) and vitamins K, C, E, and many of the B vitamins. They provide a variety of phytonutrients including beta-carotene, lutein, and zeaxanthin, which protect our cells from damage and our eyes from age-related problems, among many other effects. They also contain protein and omega-3 fats. Yes, you read that right: you can get protein and healthy fats from *plants*.

Clean Green Ingredients

Candice and Farmer Lee Jones

Let's take a closer look at the ingredients and flavors you will be using throughout this book. I want to share a little bit of background about why I've chosen them, their nutritional benefits, and how they can help to improve your whole life.

Several years ago my *Top Chef* cast mate (Season 1, baby!), Chef Lee Anne Wong, introduced me to the Chef's Garden, a family-owned organic farm in Huron, Ohio. I'll never forget that first visit: I could not believe how breathtakingly beautiful it was. Farmer Lee Jones and his family have actually built a sustainable institution for vegetables, called the Culinary Vegetable Institute. Over the past decade, Farmer Lee and his wife, Mary, have been generous enough to allow me to come back to the farm to participate in the harvest, educate myself, and cook. We shot much of this book on Farmer Lee's organic farm (a huge thank-you to Farmer Lee and Mary!). It was ridiculous fun and a great way for our team to have access to the best produce and learn more about organic farming, straight from the source. The nutritional profile and freshness of farm-to-table produce cannot be duplicated. With that in mind, let's take a closer look at what I mean by "clean greens." Whenever possible, I highly recommend purchasing seasonal, organic greens.

Super Clean Super Greens

ARUGULA: Arugula (also known as "rocket" or "wild arugula"), which you will see used in recipes throughout this book, is an edible green from the Brassicaceae family—a classification of vegetables that also includes kale, cabbage, and cauliflower. Arugula leaves are delicate and have a distinct, peppery taste. They are packed with iron for healthy red blood cells, copper, and vitamin K for strong bones and a fabulous smile!

Arugula also contains folic acid, great for moms-to-be and their growing tummies. I love using arugula to finish off soups, noodle dishes, grain recipes and, of course, it always makes for a delicious, fresh, and crisp salad.

AVOCADO: Also known as my absolute favorite food, ever. You'll find this super anti-inflammatory fruit (technically the avocado is a fruit, not a vegetable) in just about every chapter in this book. Try them in my Clean Green Guacamole and Homemade Chili-Lime Chips on page 138, use them to top your new vegan favorite, Jackfruit Curry Tacos on page 184, and toss them into my Macrobiotic Hijiki-Avocado Salad on page 116. This heart-healthy fruit is also full of natural fiber and contains high levels of vitamin E and vitamin K. Talk about an internal beauty regime! And it's packed with cancer-fighting carotenoids, which can help with overall eye health, too!

Avocados also help to support cardiovascular health and have been shown to reduce the risk of stroke and coronary artery disease. Your beautiful heart will reap the benefits of the oleic acid and omega-3 fatty acids

found in avocado, which can also help to reduce your cholesterol. Studies have shown that an avocado-rich diet improves your lipid profile.

Avocados are also a beauty food—they have been linked to promoting a healthy body weight and BMI, and those healthy fats will do wonders for your skin, hair, and nails. I eat an avocado daily. It's a way better source of vitamin E than any beauty cream. Look for semifirm avocados that are a nice dark green color. Not too hard, not too soft, but just right!

BASIL: Fresh or dried, I love adding basil to pastas, salads, dressings, pizzas, and marinades. Basil is packed with antioxidant and antibacterial properties. Fragrant, fresh basil offers a healthy amount of vitamin K, vitamin A, manganese, and magnesium. Check out my favorite recipes with basil, like the Caprese Pizza on page 220, Pasta with Sun-Dried Tomato Pesto on page 235, or just add basil leaves to your favorite juice or smoothie in the morning, or your pasta in the evening to bump up the flavor and antioxidants!

DANDELION: This beautiful yet bitter herb is delicious in smoothies and grain salads. With vitamin A for healthy eyes and vitamin C for super immunity, this super green is packed with goodness. Dandelion has been known to prevent inflammation in the body, as well as keep blood-sugar levels stable. Dandelion has also been used in natural medicine for hundreds of years to treat everything from tummy aches to fungal infections. Seek out this spectacular green fresh at the farmers' market or your local green grocer and whip up Candice's Dandelion Greens and Curry Quinoa Salad on page 110.

KALE: All hail to Mother Kale! Kale is the most-used green in this cookbook! Packed with everything from vitamin A, C, and K to mega-antioxidants and even protein, one cup of this superfood contains approximately 206 percent of your daily recommended vitamin A and approximately 134 percent of your daily recommended vitamin C intake. You will not believe that kale actually contains approximately 684 percent of your recommended vitamin K intake. Vitamin K is for "Kale" and healthy, strong bones! Kale is also a fabulous source of minerals, like potassium, iron, manganese, and phosphorus, and offers plenty of fiber and sulfur, which help to aid in digestion.

Kale is not a trend, my friends: it is here to stay. Check out the Avocado-Kale Caesar Salad on page 105, Homemade Kale Marinara Sauce on page 268, or the Kale-Mushroom Gyoza on page 199. When shopping for kale, look for firm, fresh, and crisp leaves, hard stems, and no wilting. Varieties you will find in this book include curly kale—the most common variety, as well as lacinato kale, otherwise known as Tuscan/dinosaur kale. I challenge you to eat kale on a weekly basis (I consume it daily!) and watch your body feel the difference.

MINT: One of my favorite super herbs, I adore the bright smell and flavor of mint. My mom used to make us fresh mint tea when we were kids, and I've always loved the comfort and soothing quality it provides.

Mint is a great source of copper (for beautiful hair!) and vitamin C (for super immunity) and is packed with antioxidants and natural anti-inflammatory properties. Total bonus, peppermint, mint's gorgeous sister, can also help you to breathe easier: Mint contains rosmarinic acid, which helps your cells to open air passages, resulting in clear and deep breathing.

SPINACH: Popeye's main green, spinach or baby spinach, is an edible flowering plant packed with iron, folate, manganese, and vitamins A and K. The iron in spinach helps to provide lots of oxygen for healthy muscles. This super immunity-boosting green is the most popular green used in smoothies and for juicing because it has a subtle, mild flavor, and because it's simple to measure by the handful. One handful of baby spinach is approximately 1 cup.

Add fresh baby spinach to finish off your soups, ramen, and grain recipes, or toss it into your next smoothie, and be sure to remember how truly super-packed this delicious deep green is.

SWISS CHARD: This leafy green is a member of the beet, or Chenopod family, which also includes quinoa and spinach. Mom used to cook delicious rainbow Swiss chard when we were kids, and I was always so amazed at the bright color. Chard's nutrient-packed leaves are filled with benefits like vitamins A, C, and K. One cup of Swiss chard contains 636 percent of your daily recommended value of vitamin K, amazing for strong bones and a gorgeous smile. Swiss chard is naturally filled with anti-inflammatory and antioxidant properties.

Look for chard with crisp, firm, and colorful stems, commonly found at farmers' markets and health food stores. I love Swiss chard sautéed with fruit like apples and cranberries! Try my Sautéed Swiss Chard with Apples and Sunflower Seeds on page 167.

WATERCRESS: Touted as a mega "superfood," watercress is one of the most nutrient-dense foods available to you. I love it in my salads, in homemade sushi, or atop my Japanese Okonomiyaki Savory Pancakes on page 207. Fresh watercress has a high concentration of ascorbic acid, aka vitamin C, which helps to enhance your immunity, and prevents iron deficiency. Watercress is an excellent source of vitamin K and calcium, as well. Look for crisp, long white stalks and bright green leaves.

Super Food Boosters

These all-natural miracle boosters are like nature's supplements. I love adding these super boosters to my dressings, smoothies, juices, cooking, and baked goods. They effortlessly add a boost of flavor, health benefits, and nutrients. Add them to your diet wherever you can, and reap all of the natural, healthy rewards.

APPLE CIDER VINEGAR: This stuff is the absolutely most delicious and beneficial vinegar you can find. Raw or unfiltered apple cider vinegar contains "The Mother," a cloudy web found in the vinegar, made of cellulose. Raw apple cider vinegar is derived from fresh, crushed apples, with the addition of yeast-friendly bacteria. Using a natural two-part fermentation process, the yeast-friendly bacteria changes the natural sugar from the apples into alcohol, and then into yummy vinegar with friendly good-for-you bacteria.

Raw, unfiltered apple cider vinegar is rich in natural enzymes, important minerals, and has amazing detoxifying powers. Apple cider vinegar may also help to lower LDL, aka "bad cholesterol." I love this stuff in all of my marinades, soups, and salad dressings (see page 274 for my Apple Cider Vinaigrette) and just by the spoonful. You'll notice I finish many of my soups with a cleansing ingredient. To help with digestion, try drinking a tablespoon of apple cider vinegar before each meal.

BEE POLLEN: Considered a natural "multivitamin" and used by natural health advocates, bee pollen contains vitamins, minerals, amino acids, fatty acids, enzymes, and more! Who knew? Pick up a bottle at your local health food store, and try sprinkling a teaspoon or so into your smoothies or on top of granola and yogurt. It has a mildly sweet, honey-like taste. Be sure to keep your bottle in the fridge and be mindful of individuals who may have allergies to bees.

BRAGG LIQUID AMINOS : Amino acids are the building blocks of your cells. They are the link between our food and our bodily tissues. If your body is lacking in amino acids, it can affect your physical and mental health. I love using Bragg Liquid Aminos (which tastes just like soy sauce) to finish off my cooking with an earthy and deep flavor. I also use it as a flavor booster to finish my grains, salads, lean protein, fish, stir-fries, bowls, pastas, soups, marinades, dressings, and just about anything that you need to season. Don't have Bragg Liquid Aminos on hand? Try some of these real foods that contain natural amino acids: peanuts, sesame seeds, white fish, quinoa, plant proteins, eggs, Greek or Icelandic yogurt, and organic tofu! YUM.

CAROB POWDER: Carob powder is similar to cocoa powder in flavor and texture. Derived from carob pods, carob powder is low in calories and can be substituted for cocoa in desserts and smoothies for a boost of calcium, vitamin B_2, vitamin B_6, potassium, and magnesium. Even better for the plant-based folks out there, carob is vegan and caffeine-free. Try my amazing Carob Spirulina Power Bars on page 96—the perfect energy bar for gals, busy moms, and kids on the go.

CURRY POWDER: A powerful spice blend found primarily in Indian and South Asian cuisine, curry is fragrant, delicious, and packed with powerful health benefits. I *highly* recommend cooking more with this delicious inflammation-fighting curry blend. Why? Because it's simple to sprinkle it into many recipes and it has major benefits. I love this stuff in my soups, grain salads, over eggs, and even on my homemade roasted nuts. Curry powder is usually a blend of these spices:

➤ CHILI PEPPERS: Chili peppers also contain major anti-inflammatory benefits, help with cardiovascular health, and may even clear congestion naturally.

➤ CORIANDER: Derived from the cilantro seed, coriander may help relax digestive muscles, and can help to soothe achy tummies.

➤ CUMIN: Cumin seeds are actually tiny dried fruits, and these seeds are thought to help with tummy bloat and aid digestion.

➤ FENUGREEK: Fenugreek, from the bean family, is popular in Asian and Middle Eastern cuisine. Fenugreek is loaded with fiber, protein, and iron.

➤ TURMERIC: Oh yes, my favorite of the blend, turmeric, a delicious rhizome, related to the ginger family and contains curcumin, which acts as a powerful anti-inflammatory agent. Turn to page 12 for more information on this amazing spice.

GARLIC: There's a reason why people take garlic supplements: garlic is packed with antioxidants. Garlic can help prevent and treat bacterial and fungal infections, and contains anti-inflammatory properties. Garlic is so superhuman it may also help to fight stress and fatigue and boost your immune system! Personally, I'd rather cook with it than swallow a capsule. You'll find garlic is a staple ingredient in this book, as it adds the most amazing flavor to recipes like pasta, pesto, and homemade soups.

GREEN TEA/MATCHA POWDER: The first clue that green tea is good for us: it's GREEN. Rich in antioxidants, phytonutrients, packed with vitamins C and E, green tea is a miracle elixir. I love my matcha, traditionally, as a hot tea (it helps me to relax while meditating!), in my tea cakes (see page 252), in pancakes, crepes, smoothies, and even sprinkled on fish—or try it on chocolate! Look for quality Japanese brands when it comes to green tea and matcha powder. Don't skimp . . . you deserve it!

LEMONS: With super-mega cleansing benefits, I believe that lemon water is the key to beautiful, vibrant, hydrated skin. I drink 8 to 10 cups of lemon water a day for optimum health and hydration. When your body has a cold, the healing power of lemons can work both internally, with a surge of vitamin C to defend immunity, and externally, with antiviral properties in the nose and throat. Try my super Sweet Kale Lemonade on page 56. Many of the recipes in this book contain lemon. Added to juices, dressings, marinades, salads—you name it—the taste of lemon brightens up any dish.

PLANT-BASED PROBIOTICS: Probiotics are "friendly bacteria" that help your body maintain a healthy balance of gut bacteria. Your gut bacteria, or microbiome, is involved with everything from regulating body weight to digestive health to immunity, clear skin, and even mood—so it's essential to keep it in balance.

Probiotics work by helping the body to rebuild the "beneficial flora" that are often depleted due to the effects of diet, medication, stress, and more. Fermented foods are natural probiotics: miso, pickles, and even some kefir nutmilks have probiotic powers. Fermented foods, in particular, are filled with good-for-you bacteria. Miso soup (made of fermented soybean paste) contains more than 160 healthy bacteria strains. Kombucha, yogurt, spirulina, and fermented vegetables are other good options.

Supplements work great in a pinch, but in general it's best to get your probiotics naturally. Whole foods are easy for your body to digest and the nutrients are easily absorbed by your body.

SPIRULINA: This brilliant plant-based super green is derived from blue-green algae. Considered nature's "multivitamin," spirulina is packed with protein, vitamin A, K, B$_{12}$, iron, magnesium, and even probiotics. Spirulina is widely available in both tablet and powder form. I love adding it to my smoothies, sprinkling it on my stir-fries, and adding a touch in my scrambled eggs and even my homemade pesto.

TURMERIC: This rhizome (aka root), which is native to India and used widely in Indian cooking, is derived from the *Curcuma domestica* plant. Turmeric has become popular these days for good reason: it is a natural super booster and detoxifier. Turmeric has long been used in Indian and Chinese medicine for its natural anti-inflammatory properties. Packed with manganese, iron, vitamin B$_6$, and even fiber, this is one spice you need to add to your daily routine. Try adding some to your lemon water or sprinkling a little extra turmeric (found in curry powder) on your popcorn, nuts, or Jackfruit Curry Tacos, see page 184.

Nuts and Seeds

I use a variety of nuts and seeds in my cooking. Not only do they offer texture and delicious flavor, but they are also full of protein, fiber, and healthy fats that fill you up and provide a great source of energy. For that reason, nuts and seeds are my favorite snack whenever I'm in need of a quick pick-me-up. Be sure to look for raw nuts and seeds, ditch the roasted, salted, or seasoned nuts/seeds with excess oils and crazy amounts of salt. The higher the fat content of the nut, the faster the nut will spoil, so it's important to keep nuts and seeds like walnuts, peanuts, cashews, hemp seed, flaxseed, and pistachios sealed in an airtight bag or container in the fridge, or even the freezer, to extend their shelf life. Here are a few of my favorites.

RAW WHOLE ALMONDS/ALMOND MEAL/ALMOND MILK: Just a quarter cup of almonds contains 49 percent of your daily value of biotin (no need to buy that expensive shampoo—just eat almonds!), plus vitamin E, vitamin B$_2$, copper, and manganese. The skin of the almond is rich in flavonoids, heart-healthy compounds that have fabulous antioxidant and anti-inflammatory properties. Eating almonds has been shown to reduce the risk of heart disease thanks to their abundance of vitamin E and LDL-lowering monounsaturated fats. Almonds also provide more calcium per serving than any other nut out there.

Almond milk is the perfect alternative for people who are dairy-free, and it's so easy to make yourself—check out my delicious almond milk recipe on page 264. Almonds and almond meal are also packed with monounsaturated fats, the same type of health- and beauty-promoting fats that are found in olive oil, which have been associated with reduced risk of heart disease. Almond meal or almond flour is a delicious baking swap that is gluten-free.

Talk about a super power food! When buying almonds always look for raw, which offer the most nutrients. Use them in your salads, add them to your granola, sprinkle them on yogurt, or use them as a base to make a delicious pesto (see page 235).

CASHEWS: Cashews are my favorite nut to snack on. Cashew nuts are actually seeds that grow on the bottom of the cashew apple, the fruit from the cashew tree.

Cashews contain healthy plant protein and magnesium, which help to control inflammation, give you energy, and promote bone health. I love packing up cashews to go in a mason jar before a long plane ride. They are delish roasted with a little sea salt and herbs or raw, tossed into smoothies, and/or to top off granola or even muesli. Cashews are best stored in the fridge or freezer. Check out my Clean Green Herbed Cashews for a delish treat on page 143.

CARAWAY SEEDS: Caraway seeds are full of fiber and essential minerals. Chewing caraway seeds or fennel seeds (their close sister) has long been a folk remedy for treating digestive issues (aka reducing gas!), as the oil in them is thought to relax the stomach. Caraway seeds are fantastic sprinkled on salads, roasted potatoes, and in homemade bread. Bake some up in my Potato-Onion Bread on page 176. I also love steeping caraway seeds with some fennel seeds or even some lavender for a soothing and fragrant herbal tea! Always buy the seeds whole and keep them fresh in the fridge or freezer.

CHIA SEEDS: Chia seeds have been praised for their magical properties since the days of the Aztec and Mayan warriors, who consumed them before battle (the word *chia* means "strength" in the Mayan language). Chia seeds are high in fiber and nutrient-packed. With their phosphorous and omega-3 fatty acids, these delicious, hydrating seeds can boost your brain *and* bone health. Adding chia seeds to your foods is a simple way to gain more protein for vegans and is also a simple way to improve your digestion and mental focus. Chia seeds have a mild taste and can be added to anything from morning smoothies to oatmeal to yogurt to hot grain cereals, and can be added to baked goods. Try my delish Chocolate–Almond Butter Chia Pudding on page 93.

FLAXSEED MEAL: Flaxseed meal, aka ground flaxseed, is packed with antioxidants, omega-3 fatty acids, fiber, and alpha linolenic acid (fabulous for a healthy heart and lowering bad cholesterol). Flaxseed also aids in digestion and may help relieve IBS symptoms (wow!). Always opt for ground flaxseed meal over whole flaxseeds, as your body can easily digest the nutrients in flaxseed meal, versus the whole seed. If you do purchase whole flaxseeds, you can grind them into a meal yourself by pulsing them lightly in a food processor, blender, or clean coffee grinder. I love flaxseed meal to finish off salads, in smoothies, in baked goods, to top oatmeal and hot grain cereals, or even on pasta! I add it to my marinara sauces, to thicken the sauce! Store flaxseed meal in an airtight container in the fridge.

HEMP SEEDS: Hemp seeds and marijuana come from the same species of plant, but there's no THC in hemp seeds, thus—sorry, friends—no high! But . . . your body will be high on their benefits! Hemp seed is a complete protein, meaning it offers all of the essential amino acids your body needs to fuel metabolic function and build muscle. There are five grams of lean, muscle-building protein in just two tablespoons of hemp seeds. And hemp seed is a perfect balance of omega-3 and omega-6 fatty acids, which are known to boost brain power, improve heart health, and supercharge the immune system. It's easy to find creative uses for these seeds—add them to your morning grains, hot oatmeal, a morning smoothie, homemade granola, or even a Caesar salad for an extra nutrient boost!

Hemp seeds are best raw and not toasted or salted. Store hemp seeds in the fridge or freezer in an airtight container.

PISTACHIOS: Pistachios, vibrant, tasty, and our favorite shade—green! Pistachios are packed with good-for-you monounsaturated fats and powerful antioxidants. They also contain a compound known as L-argenine, which helps to lower your blood pressure and may help to prevent blood clots. Consuming more pistachios can help to lower LDL, bad cholesterol, and they contain beneficial minerals like copper and selenium. Top off your next salad with pistachios, blend them up, and coat fish with them, snack on them when on the go, or throw them into your next smoothie.

Pistachios come shelled and unshelled; both are great options, but pistachios stay fresh for only about 3 months or so. Extend their shelf life for up to a year by freezing them!

PUMPKIN SEEDS: Also known as *pepitas*, pumpkin seeds are naturally packed with antioxidants, muscle-friendly protein, immunity-friendly zinc, and heart-happy, polyunsaturated fatty acids. Toss them into your next salad, sprinkle them on top of sautéed greens, add them to your favorite baked goods, or use them in your granola for a super nutrient boost. You can roast them up and store them at room temperature in an airtight container for two weeks. Or you can store them raw in the fridge or freezer for up to two months.

SESAME SEEDS: These seeds are loaded with vitamin E and rich in phytosterols that may help to lower LDL cholesterol. Sesame seeds come in pretty shades of black, yellow, brown, and red. If you buy them raw, be sure to toast them before using to bring out their incredible nutty flavor. You can even add toasted sesame seeds to a food processor and create a quick tahini paste for making hummus. Yum! Sesame is used in my favorite, Asian cuisine, and their flavor pairs perfectly with Japanese-inspired recipes, like sushi, okonomiyaki, my Kale-Mushroom Gyoza on page 199 or the Asian Ginger Steak Salad on page 196. Sesame seeds should be 100 percent dry when purchased. Any moisture in the container that sesame seeds are stored in can make them turn rancid. Store them in a cool, dry, and dark place, ideally in the fridge or freezer.

SUNFLOWER SEEDS: Sunflower seeds are a delicious way to get vitamins B, E, folic acid, and fatty acids. They make for a very satisfying snack, and are also great tossed into any raw salad. Sunflower nut butter, aka "sunbutter," is a delicious alternative for those with a peanut allergy.

You can store roasted sunflower seeds in a airtight container for 2 weeks at room temperature, You can also freeze and store raw sunflower seeds in an airtight container for up to 1 year.

WALNUTS: Walnuts are a perfect source of omega-3 fatty acids, essential acids our body needs to get from food sources because we can't naturally produce them. The omega-3s in walnuts are brain-boosters, improving memory and overall cognitive function, as well as lowering your risk for Alzheimer's disease. Break them into pieces and add some of these flavorful anti-inflammatory nuts to your smoothies, desserts, or oatmeal for a nice nutty flavor and a hint of crunch. When purchasing, look for raw walnuts—you can buy them whole or in pieces, depending on your needs (walnut pieces will save you some $$). The "skin" on the walnut should not appear dry. The best way to maintain the fresh taste of walnuts is to store them in an airtight container at room temperature for 3 months, or in the fridge for approximately 6 months or in the freezer for up to 1 year.

Herbs and Spices

Spices offer a potent way to brighten, flavor, and enhance any dish with just a pinch. But there's a lot more to spices than their flavor alone—they also offer a host of nutritional and healing benefits. Try adding some cinnamon to your coffee to prevent inflammation, or some paprika in your soups to add a touch of vitamin A. I've also added a few unique spice blends from Japan and the Middle East, so you can open up your palate and bring the world into your kitchen.

BLACK PEPPERCORN: This commonly used spice may aid in the prevention and treatment of an array of health issues, from arthritis and high blood pressure to constipation and indigestion. Black pepper can help with digestion, as it stimulates the taste buds and also boosts the amount of hydrochloric acid in the body. With its high levels of manganese and vitamin K, black pepper can also help with strong bones and healthy skin.

Freshly ground black pepper adds a distinctive kick to almost any dish. Invest in a good pepper mill, purchase whole peppercorns, and grind as needed. Crack some on top of your salads or soups, fish or eggs!

CAYENNE: Cayenne is a member of the genus *Capsicum L.* commonly known as chile peppers. Made from pure red cayenne chile peppers that have been dried and ground into a fine powder, cayenne packs a lot of heat, so a little goes a long way. Cayenne peppers are high in capsaicin, a compound that is thought to help reduce inflammation and increase blood flow (good for you-know-what!). Sprinkle a little cayenne into your lemon water for a fiery lemonade, or add it to your favorite Mexican dishes for heat! I love finishing my shrimp tacos, burritos, and tostadas with a little hint of cayenne.

CINNAMON: Derived from the bark of a tree, this sweet-tasting spice offers antioxidant and antiseptic benefits and can help with nausea and other digestive problems. Cinnamon contains calcium and fiber and also helps to stabilize blood sugar. Try sprinkling cinnamon into your coffee grinds in

the a.m. or stir it into a hot bowl of oats topped with yogurt to reap all its health benefits and add a hint of earthy sweetness.

CUMIN: A delicious spice commonly used in Southwestern and Mexican cuisine, cumin is loaded with impressive medicinal qualities that may help to prevent cancer and fight diabetes! Cumin contains iron, manganese, and copper. I love adding cumin to my marinades, chili, roasted nuts, soups, marinades, and sauces. Recent studies show that cumin may also aid in weight loss by revving up your metabolism.

DILL: Commonly associated with German, Polish, and Ukrainian cuisines, dill seeds are stronger and more flavorful than the leaves themselves. Dill's green leaves are soft and wispy with a sweet taste. The health benefits come from flavonoids (powerful compounds with antibacterial properties). Whenever possible, choose fresh over dried for the best flavor. You'll find dill pairs perfectly with salmon and is a fabulous pick for dips and dressings.

GARLIC POWDER: Sweet, sweet garlic powder, you'll find it throughout this cookbook. As we've already discussed, garlic offers a ton of anti-inflammatory and antiviral benefits, including super-cancer-fighting powers. Garlic powder is made from dehydrated garlic that has been ground into a powder. It adds mega flavor to recipes with no extra fat or calories.

GINGER: One of my favorite spices, ginger is full of anti-inflammatory benefits and also helps soothe an unhappy tummy. Look for fresh ginger, and grate it in marinades, soups, and salad dressings. Ginger tea is also delicious and so soothing. My Japanese grandfather (*Jiichan!*) used to grate fresh ginger into many of his recipes for optimum health and digestion.

LAVENDER: Sweet lavender, how you are my favorite herb. Lavender isn't just for potions and soaps—it adds a fabulously fragrant floral note to homemade herbal tea (add some fennel seeds, too!), homemade lavender honey, and—um, yes!—it really is the ultimate relaxing ingredient for an all-natural bath soak.

Lavender oil is believed to have antiseptic and anti-inflammatory properties that can be used to help heal minor wounds. Research has also revealed that the essential oil of lavender can help in treating anxiety, depression, and sleeplessness.

NUTMEG: Nutmeg is the pit or seed of the nutmeg tree. It has a sweet, earthy, and somewhat bitter taste that pairs well with cinnamon. Nutmeg is packed with anti-inflammatory properties. Healthy trace minerals, naturally found in nutmeg, include: potassium, manganese, iron, and calcium. Nutmeg oil has shown to aid in brain function and protect from degenerative diseases like Alzheimer's. Don't forget a magic sprinkle of nutmeg also has antioxidants like beta-carotene and vitamin C! I recommend buying nutmeg whole and grating it on a microplane as needed—fresh nutmeg has a strong flavor, so a little sprinkle will usually do. I add nutmeg to my coffee every day and also use it in my baked goods and in granolas and muesli.

OREGANO: Frequently used in Italian cooking, oregano is a fragrant herb that has been shown to have some incredible health benefits. Oregano oil (found in fresh oregano) contains antibacterial, antiviral, and antifungal properties. Oregano, or oregano oil, may also help you to relax and calm your mind, nerves, or sore muscles. I generally prefer dried oregano for cooking, as it is more potent than fresh and has a long shelf life.

PAPRIKA: Paprika is a hot and beneficial spice derived from the fruit of the bell pepper. Paprika is loaded with carotenoids—the pigments that give it its beautiful red hue. Its lutein and zeaxanthin content benefits your beautiful eyes, and its high content of vitamin A (1 tablespoon contains more than 100 percent of your daily requirement) helps to maintain cell health. I love this stuff on roasted potatoes, sprinkled into pea soup, and whisked into salad dressings that need a little extra flavor! Try it smoked or sweet— each has its own unique flavor.

PUMPKIN PIE SPICE: A perfect pairing of cinnamon, ginger, nutmeg, cloves, and allspice, pumpkin pie spice is wildly popular during the fall and winter months and is full of antioxidant and anti-inflammatory properties. We've already covered the benefits of cinnamon, ginger, and nutmeg, but allspice and cloves also offer nutrition along with their deliciously warm, spicy flavor.

ALLSPICE: Made from a dried unripe berry of the Caribbean evergreen tree, allspice is the secret ingredient in Jamaican jerk cooking! Allspice is fabulously potent and packed with 25 active phenols—a category of antioxidant that may lower your cholesterol and blood pressure.

CLOVES: Cloves also come from the evergreen tree. Packed with manganese, which helps with healthy bones and skin and also protects against free-radical damage, whole and ground cloves are delicious in teas, spiced wine, and baked goods.

ROSEMARY: When cooking with delicate rosemary, your entire home will smell of its delightful, woodsy aroma. Rosemary's potent essence alone may help with blood flow to your brain and is thought to help improve memory. But eating it is even better—rosemary contains fiber, B vitamins, and antioxidants.

You can buy rosemary dried or fresh—if you are using it right away, I highly recommend buying fresh. I love using rosemary and olive oil for roasting root vegetables. It is also fabulous finely chopped and sprinkled over pasta and potatoes.

SUMAC: This popular spice used in Middle Eastern cuisine is derived from ground dark-reddish-colored berries. Sumac is quickly becoming popular due to its super-unique tart flavor. There really isn't anything quite like it; I suggest you give it a try next time you're looking to add a new flavor to fish or lean meat. Add it to a salad dressing or spinkle it on a hearty grain salad or a hot soup. Look for this unique spice at your Middle Eastern cook shop.

THYME: Thyme is a powerful and natural antiseptic herb that contains antioxidants and anti-inflammatory properties. It has long been used in folk remedies to relieve the symptoms of chest colds. Thyme has a distinct and delicate flavor that is delicious in roasted chicken, stirred into soups and sauces, or paired with roasted squash or potatoes. I recommend using fresh thyme versus dried.

TOGARASHI : Togarashi is a Japanese spice blend of chili pepper, orange peel, black sesame seeds, white sesame seeds, Japanese pepper, ginger, and seaweed. Also known as shichimi togarashi, or "seven-spice blend," it offers many of the same benefits as chili pepper and cayenne—a speedy metabolism and increase in blood flow. I love this spice sprinkled over my ramen, soba noodles, okonomiyaki, and other Japanese dishes.

ZA'ATAR: This Middle Eastern spice blend is made up of sumac (see page 22), sesame seeds, thyme, oregano, and on occasion salt. I highly recommend making your own za'atar spice at home. Add it to your hummus recipes, season meats and lean proteins with it, use it to flavor Greek yogurt and olive oil for a delicious dip, or even add some to bread dough and bake for a super-flavorful flatbread.

Flours

Pasta is amazing, and bread, cookies, and cakes are always going to be a part of our culture. But the more we learn about the long-term health effects of gluten—the protein found in wheat, rye, and barley that has been linked to chronic inflammation—the more important it is to eat these foods in *moderation*. Fortunately, for those with gluten sensitivities or even celiac disease, a wide variety of gluten-free flours are available that make for simple, nutritious swaps. Almond meal, coconut, and garbanzo bean flours are just three examples.

There are no hard-and-fast rules about flours in this book. I've included recipes that utilize all kinds of flours—white rice and semolina. All flours contain nutrients, and some, such as coconut flour, contain high amounts of healthy dietary fiber. Whole-wheat flour, for example, is rich in vitamins, folate, riboflavin, and vitamins B_1, B_3, and B_5. Try spelt, semolina, or rice flour, or my new fave, coconut flour, and then choose a flour that works best for you. Here's a little more on the flours you'll find in my recipes:

ALL-PURPOSE FLOUR: All-purpose flour, most commonly used for baking, is a blend of low-gluten soft wheat plus high-gluten hard wheat. It doesn't contain the germ or the bran, thus it is enriched with nutrients and vitamins artificially, after it has been processed. I don't like to use white flour often because it contains gluten and has little nutritive value, but in some recipes (especially for baked goods), it does produce a much better result than alternative flours.

ALMOND MEAL/FLOUR: When some of my cruelty-free friends introduced me to vegan baking years ago, I couldn't believe how incredibly delicious and moist the results were. After I began to see the health benefits of a vegetarian-based diet, I began to swap many of my baking recipes over to the vegan side. Almond flour is a great way to add some texture (plus protein and fiber) to any baked good.

Almond flour is made with blanched almonds (skins removed), whereas almond meal can be made either with whole or blanched almonds. Compared to other nuts, almonds provide the most calcium and are beneficial for heart health and lowering cholesterol. Almond meal can easily be made in your food processor; just grab some blanched almonds and throw them into a high-powered blender or food processor and grind to a fine meal. Don't mix too much, or you'll get almond butter! I use almond meal in my vegan cakes, pancakes, and cookies.

COCONUT FLOUR: Coconut flour is a light, fluffy flour that is delicious in baking recipes. It lends a bit of coconut essence to whatever you're baking, but is unsweetened and low in sugar. Made of defatted coconut meat that has been dried and ground, it is high in fiber, naturally gluten-free, and low in carbs. Coconut flour is an exceptionally fabulous source of manganese, which helps to keep your skin gorgeous and your bones healthy. Total bonus, it also contains almost twice as much protein as whole-wheat flour.

To try it out in your favorite baking recipe, replace ¼ cup (per 1 cup) of regular flour with coconut flour. You'll get more filling fiber and protein into your pancakes, crepes, cakes, and treats!

GARBANZO BEAN FLOUR: Garbanzo bean (chickpea) flour is gluten-free and contains more protein and fiber than conventional all-purpose flour. When used for baking, try substituting this delicious iron-packed flour in some of your favorite recipes (the conversion is the same, cup for cup). I use gluten-free flour in my Homemade Coconut Cake (page 259) and Vegan Dark Chocolate–Avocado Cake (page 248) recipes.

SEMOLINA FLOUR: Semolina, derived from durum wheat, is full of iron, magnesium, and folate and is loaded with protein. Semolina flour is often used in traditional Italian pasta making, and results in a soft, tender, delicate pasta.

SPELT FLOUR: Spelt flour, derived from an ancient form of wheat, is great for baking flat breads, pie crusts, and earthy-flavored pancakes. Spelt flour is high in niacin, which is great for boosting your metabolism. It is also full of important minerals needed for optimum health, like iron, zinc, and magnesium. If you are using all-purpose flour, try substituting with 50 percent spelt flour to increase the nutrient value of your breads. Note that spelt does contain gluten.

WHITE RICE FLOUR: With a distinct rice flavor and a soft and fluffy texture, rice flour has long been used in Japanese cuisine, and is now popular in gluten-free baking. White rice flour is a fabulous option because it is low in fat, high in carbohydrates, and easier to digest than wheat flour. Rice flour has a mild yet refined, distinct taste, perfect for baked goods. When I was growing up my mom made homemade *mochi* with *kinako* (sweetened, roasted soybean flour) using rice flour. Now I use it in everything from my Pumpkin Mochi Tea Cake (page 245) to my delicious mochi cookies!

WHOLE-WHEAT FLOUR: Whole-wheat flour is similar to all-purpose flour, but is less processed—the germ, bran, and endosperm remain intact. Whole-wheat flour has a slightly nutty flavor and it contains natural oils, so it is best to store it in the fridge. As you might expect, whole-wheat flour is packed with more nutrients than refined white flour, including protein, calcium, and iron. Try making pizza dough, breads, muffins, or pancakes with whole-wheat flour.

Grains

Move over, meat: it's time for protein-packed grains to take center stage. Studies show that eating more grains like quinoa, barley, farro, and amaranth can boost energy and have even been associated with longer lifespans. Replacing meat with grains that have a high protein-to-carbohydrate ratio is best. These include barley, freekeh, quinoa, and oats. Quinoa is technically a seed but it is consumed like a grain. It contains 8 grams of protein per cup, and essential amino acids. Amaranth and freekeh are also fantastic options: 1 cup of either, cooked, contains 9 grams of protein. Try out some of these main grains for breakfast, a protein power-packed lunch, or a satisfying dinner.

AMARANTH: This gluten-free, versatile grain can be prepared sweet, for breakfast, or savory, for dinner. Amaranth is actually a "pseudo-cereal" grain-like seed; related to the quinoa, beet, chard, and spinach family, it's naturally packed with protein, vitamin B$_6$, calcium, and potassium. My Greek Yogurt and Amaranth Berry Porridge on page 94 is a delicious way to start eating this healthy grain.

BARLEY: With a nutty, earthy flavor, a "pasta-like" consistency, and a powerhouse nutritional profile, barley is a clear swap from your plain old boring rice dish. Barley contains manganese, selenium, fiber, copper, B vitamins, phosphorus, magnesium, and more. Barley can also help aid in digestion due to its fiber content. Barley is delicious tossed into salads, soups, and even veggie burgers.

BROWN RICE: Brown rice is the same grain as white rice, but is the least processed version of the plant, with the hull and bran intact. It's these parts of the grain that contain the protein, thiamine, calcium, magnesium, fiber, and potassium. Some clever and fun new ways to swap in brown rice for white: sushi rolls, brown rice and beans, brown fried rice, in a clean green bowl with avocado, edamame, lemon, and soy sauce (yum!), or tossed into any leftovers to create a full meal stir-fry.

FARRO: Farro is a delicious ancient grain from the Middle East, wildly popular today in Italy, Europe, and Asia. I love farro—it is earthy, delicious, and packed with fiber, protein, magnesium, and vitamins B and E. I like to toss this wild grain into my salads and soups. A farro salad makes for a perfect post-workout lean lunch, or for a filling dinner. There is a Kale Fried "Rice" recipe with farro that you must try on page 215.

FREEKEH: Freekeh, another Middle Eastern grain, is made from green wheat that undergoes a roasting process, which imparts a smoky, nutty flavor. With its nutrient-dense profile and ease in cooking (think rice or pasta), freekeh is quickly becoming one of the next big "superfoods." Freekeh is high in protein and fiber as well as minerals like iron and magnesium. Try it in place of couscous or quinoa in your next grain main meal.

QUINOA (RED AND WHITE): This wildly popular "grain" is actually a seed. Quinoa is a complete protein, meaning that it contains all of the essential amino acids your body needs. High in protein, B vitamins, iron, and phosphorus, quinoa also packs plenty of fiber and is very filling. Quinoa comes in many colors, and all of them are delicious. I like to use this super-versatile, mega-nutritious seed in soups, salads, and even as a breakfast porridge.

ROLLED OATS: Who doesn't love oats? From oatmeal to granola to muesli, oats are a breakfast favorite. Whole rolled oats are packed with nutrition, including plenty of water-soluble dietary fiber. Studies show that eating a diet rich in whole grains, like oats, may help lower cholesterol and decrease your chance of developing breast cancer and type 2 diabetes. Always look for rolled oats in bulk bins. I love using oats in my Bircher Muesli on page 79, and hot in the morning over the stovetop with a touch of brown sugar, bananas, and raw walnuts.

Beans and Legumes

Beans and legumes are another great source of plant-based protein and are inexpensive, versatile, and widely available. The carbs found in beans and legumes are rich in fiber, magnesium, iron, and potassium, which help lower bad LDL cholesterol and blood pressure. The healthy soluble fiber in beans and legumes is helpful for anyone trying to maintain a healthy weight. Try out a few favorites below and find out for yourself just how fab beans and legumes can be.

ADZUKI BEANS: Also known as azuki beans, this beautiful red bean hasn't been popular in the United States until recently. But just 1 cup of these beans is loaded with 25 percent of your daily value for iron, 30 percent of your magnesium, 25 percent of your potassium, and a whopping 70 percent of your daily recommended folic acid. Adzuki beans are used frequently in Japanese cooking, traditionally served with rice, and also made into sweet bean pastes to fill mochi and Japanese pastries. I love my adzuki beans in macrobiotic salads as well as rice dishes. Call me biased, but this is my favorite bean! You can find adzuki beans dried or canned. Be sure to rinse and drain canned beans to remove excess salt.

BLACK BEANS: Protein-packed black beans are rich in anti-inflammatory flavonoids. One cup of iron- and calcium-loaded black beans contains a boatload (15 grams!) of fiber. I like using black beans in my Latin American–inspired dishes—try them with the Chili-Lime Shrimp Tostadas on page 204. Or create a bean and grain salad with a combo of farro, black beans, fresh greens, and a clean homemade vinaigrette from Chapter 14.

CANNELLINI BEANS: Often found in Italian cooking, cannellini beans are naturally detoxifying due to their high content of molybdenum—a compound that stimulates detoxifying enzymes. These beans are perfect for adding some protein to clean soups and salads. Add them to your next wild arugula and red onion salad, or make a delish three-bean side salad with a simple lemon vinaigrette!

EDAMAME (SOY BEANS): Edamame contains vitamin A, iron, magnesium, copper, potassium, and more. Soy's major benefits come from its content of isoflavones, which may help to fight cancer and osteoporosis. Always opt for organic or fermented soy (tofu, miso, tempeh) when possible. Hey, let's chat about soy, shall we? So, there's a natural presence of isoflavones in soybeans. These are compounds that minimize the effects of estrogen in the body. Eating soy in moderate amounts is considered healthy.

There is a concern that high estrogen levels are linked to an increased risk of breast cancer, though the science is still new. The best choice when it comes to soy is always fermented or organic. It tastes great, is easy to digest, and is full of plant protein. And a key rule to remember in clean eating is that the closer the food is to the source—in the case of plants, that's the soil—the more nutrition there is.

GARBANZO BEANS: Also known as "chickpeas," the garbanzo is actually a legume and one of the most popular in the world. Garbanzo beans are packed with folate, protein, fiber, and calcium. Try them in delicious homemade hummus, dips, or, my favorite, my Vegan Chickpea Curry Burgers on page 150.

GREEN BEANS: Green beans are wildly popular and found almost all over the world. Cook up this delicious green veggie for immunity-boosting vitamin C and vitamin K. I love to eat them steamed with just a touch of olive oil and sea salt. Add them to your Niçoise salads or pair them with my Miso-Orange Glazed Salmon on page 202.

These beans are always best fresh, but when not available, you can find them frozen or canned—just be sure to look for "no salt added" on the label.

KIDNEY BEANS: Delicious kidney beans are a naturally detoxifying food, packed with protein and fiber. One cup of kidney beans provides approximately 13.5 grams of protein and 16.5 grams of fiber. If you purchase them canned, be sure to go for low or no salt added, drain the beans, and rinse them twice. The liquid in the can of beans can cause tummy problems, like bloating and gas (oh, my!).

I like to toss kidney beans into my minestrone soup, add them to any whole-grain bowl, or toss them into white or brown rice for a beautiful, filling side dish.

LENTILS: Lentils are packed with soluble fiber, which breaks down easily in your body and helps to lower LDL cholesterol. Lentils have also been linked to heart health due to their high content of folate and magnesium. A favorite of many vegetarians, and my dad, lentils are super-quick and easy to prepare in soups, dips, lentil cakes, and vegan recipes. You'll find many delish recipes with lentils throughout this book, including my Red Lentil Soup on page 125.

PEAS: Delicious, bright green peas are my new favorite way to get more protein, fiber, and vitamins A and C. Fresh peas are delicious in vegetable and grain salads, as well as soups. Try them in my Creamy Coconut and Fresh Pea Mint Soup on page 129. Buying fresh peas is really worth the expense—especially if they are the star of a dish. But if they're out of season, or just too expensive, frozen peas will work just fine. They retain a great deal of their nutrients, and are easy to keep on hand in the freezer for anytime you need them.

PEANUTS: This super-popular "nut" is actually a legume, as it grows in the soil instead of on a tree. Peanuts not only offer 7 grams of protein per serving, they are also full of niacin/vitamin B, which is recommended for an energy boost and major antioxidant protection.

Be sparing on the peanuts, though, as they are high in fat and calories. (As Julia Child was famous for saying, "Everything in moderation, including moderation.") Try peanuts whipped into a smoothie, toss them into your granola bar recipes, and make your own healthy peanut butter by adding peanuts to your food processor for a whirl. Purchase peanuts raw and unsalted for more nutritional benefits.

SUGAR SNAP PEAS AND SNOW PEAS: Snap peas are delicious round pods that are low in calories and high in nutrients, like vitamins C and A. The snow pea is a flat pea pod, also full of vitamin C, antioxidants, and iron.

Always purchase both varieties of peas fresh, and store them in the fridge for up to 5 days. Try adding them to the Asian Ginger Steak Salad on page 196, or sauté them with some avocado oil, orange zest, and tamari soy sauce. YUM!

Sugar

Time to cut it DOWN! We eat a ton of sugar in America—literally. The average American eats more than 150 pounds of sugar each year! That's almost 21 million tons of sugar! But most of that sugar isn't consumed from the sugar bowl—it is hidden in processed foods. Added sugars can be found in everything from tomato sauce, soups, and dressings to crackers and breads. And then, of course, there are the packaged cookies, soda, candy, and pastries we consume. . . . Oh, dear.

One way to wean yourself off sugar is to stop eating so many processed foods—make your own sauces, dressings, and soups from scratch. Empower yourself, cook more, and take control of what you eat. And when it comes to indulging your sweet tooth every once in a while, make your treats with natural sweeteners instead of refined sugar. Never reach for fake, processed sweeteners. Remember, knowledge is power; educate yourself on what you are putting into that beautiful body. Here are a few naturally sweet options, if you must:

AGAVE NECTAR: This syrupy sweetener has a mild and naturally sweet flavor. Agave is high in fructose, a fruit sugar linked to weight gain and liver problems, so health experts do not recommend it. If you bake with agave, there is one important thing to note: It is approximately one and a half times as sweet as sugar, so a little goes a long way. Be smart and use it sparingly.

BROWN RICE SYRUP: I love making my granola bars, cakes, and cookies with this natural, earthy sweetener. It adds moisture as well as sweetness to most baked goods. Some rice syrups are made with a combination of barley and rice and thus are not totally gluten-free, so make sure to read the label when you buy it. Brown rice syrup will keep for up to 1 year in a cool, dry place.

BROWN SUGAR: Brown sugar is natural white cane sugar with added molasses. I often prefer it in my baked goods, such as my banana chocolate chip cookies, Dark Chocolate–Avocado Brownies (see page 248), and in my morning oats, barbecue sauces, marinades, rubs, and even chiles. Again, just like white sugar (and any sweetener on this list), use in moderation!

COCONUT SUGAR: Coconut sugar and coconut palm sugar are derived from the sap of a coconut palm tree. Coconut sugar has a rich caramel color and tastes similar to brown sugar, with a slight coconut note. Coconut sugar is minimally processed compared to some other heavily processed sugars.

Note: *Coconut palm sugar* and *palm sugar* are not the same thing. One is derived from the sugar palm tree and the other from the coconut palm. Coconut sugar contains a small amount of nutrients plus minerals; like iron, magnesium, zinc, and potassium. It also contains some B vitamins (B_1, B_2, B_3, and B_6). Try swapping in coconut sugar, cup for cup, for regular white sugar in your baking!

HONEY: One of my favorite ways to sweeten tea, cakes, and my homemade Green Granola Bars on page 73 is by using a touch of honey. Honey is derived from flower nectar, and since there are obviously thousands of different flowers, there are thousands of different honey varieties out there. Here are a few of the ones you'll find most often:

➤ CLOVER: Light color, mild taste, most common

➤ ORANGE BLOSSOM: Light color, citrus flavor

➤ WILDFLOWER: Dark color, flavors vary

Honey has long been used in homeopathic remedies, and has antibacterial and anti-inflammatory properties. The darker the honey, the higher the levels of antioxidants. Try to purchase grade-A honey when possible and support your local beekeeper.

RAW HONEY: Raw honey is an unprocessed honey, which contains more nutrients than regular honey. Raw honey means that it has not been heated

or filtered. Raw honey may contain trace amounts of pollen grains that are removed during the processing of honey, which is why some people believe it's superior to regular honey. But the difference is minuscule.

Raw honey, like all honey, contains natural antibacterial properties. I love to use raw honey in baking, and in my marinades and homemade dressings.

MANUKA HONEY: Manuka honey is collected in New Zealand from honey bees that pollenate from the Manuka tree. More antibacterial properties are found in manuka honey than any other type of honey. Manuka honey contains methylglyoxal (MG), an antibacterial compound that is found in most honey, but manuka is packed with it. Some people believe there is a medical/home remedy use for manuka honey, to help treat minor scrapes, cuts, burns, and wounds.

I love to smear a touch of manuka honey on my Green Matcha Tea Loaf Cake on page 252 or my Pumpkin Mochi Tea Cake on page 245.

MOLASSES/BLACKSTRAP MOLASSES: Molasses is the dark liquid by-product leftover from refining white table sugar. Blackstrap molasses is made from the third boiling of the sugar, and thus becomes a super-concentrated by-product. Molasses is the most nutrient-based sweetener you can find, containing vitamins and minerals, such as iron, calcium, manganese, copper, potassium, magnesium, selenium, and vitamin B_6.

Molasses has a deep, rich taste that pairs well with earthy, spicy baked goods, like gingerbread; it is also great for savory marinades and barbecue sauces.

TURBINADO SUGAR/RAW SUGAR: A delicious, minimally processed sweetener that makes for a delightful and natural sprinkle-like topping to cupcakes and scones. I love making honey-roasted sweet and salty nuts with a little raw sugar. Raw sugar comes from the first stage of the cane sugar refining process. It contains higher molasses content with a lovely light brown color. I find that many friends love this sweetener in their coffee and tea, as well. You can usually find it for sale in bulk, which helps to offset the slightly higher price.

Super Clean Detox Foods

Some of my favorite foods also happen to be great natural detoxifiers. I try to incorporate a few of these ingredients into my meals every day. It's easy! For instance, you can go for a morning smoothie with avocado and grapefruit on the side, a lunch of kale salad or a cabbage cilantro slaw, made with a lemon–olive oil vinaigrette, and finish the day off with a miso-glazed salmon, a side of sautéed collard greens, and fresh melon slices for dessert. The cleaner and greener you eat, the cleaner and greener you will feel. Consider purchasing these foods and stock up your pantry/fridge with these clean eating essentials for a clean green life!

AVOCADO: Yes, I am listing avocado again, because they may be the most fabulous food on this planet. I try to consume this beauty fruit just about daily, and I'll find any excuse or recipe to use it. Whip up some of my guacamole on page 138, try it in the Avocado-Kale Caesar Salad on page 105, or swap avocado for banana in your next smoothie (as an added benefit, your smoothie will be lower in sugar!).

CABBAGE: This colorful vegetable is a natural diuretic that can help to cleanse your body of excess liquid, carrying toxins along with it. It's also rich in sulfur, which studies have shown can help your liver break down toxins so they're easily flushed away. Another reason to love cabbage: it's super inexpensive, close to 99 cents a head in most places, and it tops any taco, burrito, and even my Japanese pancake—"okonomiyaki"—recipe perfectly. Look for firm, crisp green or purple varieties.

CILANTRO: Love it or hate it, cilantro's natural oils may help to promote digestion and alleviate tummy aches. Cilantro's strong flavor is perfect paired with mild avocado, to top off Asian or Southeast Asian dishes, and, of course, is delish in Mexican-inspired recipes! Try cilantro leaves to top off the Chili-Lime Shrimp Tostadas on page 204.

COCONUT OIL: When used in moderation, unrefined coconut oil is a delicious, fragrant gift from gorgeous Mama Nature. With its concentration of MCTs (medium chain triglycerides), unrefined coconut oil, in moderate amounts, may help you lower cholesterol and maintain a healthy weight and flat tummy. I recommend using coconut oil in moderation in place of butter when cooking Thai- or Indian-inspired recipes and baking treats. Enjoy the rich, luscious flavors unrefined coconut oil brings to your favorite recipes. I also recommend adding coconut oil to your daily natural beauty routine by using it to gently remove eye makeup or to shave or soften your legs; you can even use 1 teaspoon as a deep conditioner for 5 minutes with a damp hair towel. Rinse well. Gorgeous from the inside out!

COLLARD GREENS: Collard greens can help to lower your LDL "bad" cholesterol levels and help to aid in superdigestion! Like kale, they are a green with some heft, and stand up to steaming well. Collards are also great tossed into soups and delicious hefty grain salads.

EXTRA-VIRGIN OLIVE OIL: Full of antioxidants and vitamin E, olive oil also helps to reduce inflammation in the body. Research suggests olive oil phenols can get rid of free radicals in your body. I say, cook with this stuff every day. Remember to purchase first-pressed high-quality extra-virgin olive oil versus regular olive oil for the most health benefits, and use it often in salads, as some of its beneficial properties are lost when olive oil is heated.

GRAPEFRUIT: Fabulous Fruit Fact: Grapefruit's Latin name is *citrus paradisi*. Maybe that's because this citrus fruit will put your beautiful body in paradise: Just one grapefruit will give you more than half your daily requirement for vitamin C. The pink shade of grapefruit comes from the phytonutrient lycopene, which is a powerful free-radical fighter. Grapefruit contains a soluble fiber called pectin (also found in apples, lemons, and oranges), and can help lower cholesterol. When purchasing, avoid grapefruit with soft spots; look for a firm citrus peel that's smooth in texture. Segment out a few grapefruits for a super-detox salad and go crazy with your juicer—it is absolutely perfect in juices.

KALE: Super beauty kale, my absolute favorite green in this book, is also one of the cleanest, most popular antioxidant-packed greens available. As we've discussed, kale is chock-full of vitamin K and many other vitamins and nutrients. If you are detoxing from dairy, be sure to eat your calcium-rich kale in its place!

LEMON WATER: I recommend drinking water with a squeeze of fresh lemon all day, every day: try to sip on 8 to 10 glasses throughout the day. Lemons are full of powerful antioxidants that may stimulate liver enzymes to help flush toxins from your body. Grab a reusable bottle or a mason jar and squeeze the lemon into your water, releasing the juice, and then add the whole wedges to the water, if using organic lemons. If you're using conventional lemons, simply add the juice and go!

MELON: Melons are packed with hydrating nutrients, electrolytes, and very few calories. They are rich in potassium and vitamin C and have a high water content, making them a natural diuretic. When shopping for melons, look for fruit that is firm and ripe with no bruising; heavy is good. Tap the melon and listen for a hollow sound, or smell the melon around its stem area—you want a melon with a fresh, fragrant scent.

Add some melon into your day with my simple Cucumber Aloe Melon Juice on page 60.

MISO PASTE: Miso fabulous! Miso is made from fermented soybeans and contains good-for-your-tummy probiotic benefits. It's also naturally loaded with protein, iron, vitamin B$_6$, and magnesium. Ranging from light-bodied "Shiro Miso" (White Miso) to dark, rich, umami "Aka Miso" (Red Miso), miso paste adds depth of flavor to marinades, soups, sauces, and glazes and is very popular in Japanese cooking. I grew up eating miso soup for breakfast in Japan and loved every "umami" moment of it. Try it with some white rice and fermented pickles on the side. YUM.

I prefer red miso to white and often use the organic brand Marukome. Miso is best stored in an airtight container in the fridge. Try cooking with miso in my Miso-Orange Glazed Salmon on page 202 or my Creamy Miso Dressing on page 272.

RADISH: These gorgeous little bulbs contain glucosinolates—properties that may help with your body's natural detoxification process. I love thinly slicing radishes on a mandoline and adding them to salads, or placing them beautiful and whole on crudité platters to eat with hummus and a touch of za'atar spice or dipping them into a creamy tahini dip. YUM.

WILD SALMON: I am truly a wild salmon lover! Packed with heart-healthy, inflammation-fighting omega-3 fatty acids and delicious bone-strengthening and immunity-boosting vitamin D, wild salmon is one seriously amazing fish.

Wild is always the best option when choosing salmon. Why? Because wild salmon is leaner, containing half the fat of farmed salmon, and also contains more nutrients than farmed salmon. Farm-raised salmon have also been found to contain higher levels of pollutants like PCBs, and may be fed antibiotics. Try cooking with wild salmon in my Coconut Curry Salmon Salad on page 112 or my Chipotle Salmon Burger on page 153 or even with my Smashed Avocado and Smoked Salmon over Pumpernickel on page 161. A great rule of thumb to remember when shopping: "Fish don't belong on farms."

Look for the following symbols at the top of each recipe to help you find the dishes that match your dietary goals. Also keep in mind that most recipes in this book can be modified to be dairy- and gluten-free.

- Vegetarian
- Vegan
- Gluten-Free
- Dairy-Free
- Low Sugar

2

THE CLEAN GREEN
CLEANSE

All of the recipes in this book were developed to be clean, green, and packed with both taste and nutrition. I don't believe in counting calories so I don't offer a calorie count with each recipe as clean eating is a lifestyle, not a diet. Of course, some foods, no matter how nutritious, can impact your weight more than others. So with that in mind, I put together a guide for you, a two-week Clean Green Cleanse for those times when you're looking to detox from a period of more indulgent eating, rev up your weight loss, and reset your taste buds.

This cleanse is not a diet and it is not a fast. It is a meal plan that offers two full weeks of clean eating, using the recipes in this book. You will start each day with a simple-to-make, delicious, filling, and low-sugar green smoothie, followed by a cleansing lunch packed with powerful green detoxifying ingredients like seaweed, leeks, kale, and avocado (for a complete list of my favorite detoxifying foods, turn to pages 39–42). Your dinner will harness the power of plant protein for hearty bowls and salads that are meat-free and allow your digestive system to take a rest from the energy-consuming job of processing animal protein. Hell yeah. It's also very important to take a plant-based probiotic twice a day during this cleanse period. I recommend doing so even after these two weeks for a happy, healthy tummy.

Finally, be sure to cut out *all* processed foods and sugars (yes, that means your favorite coffee creamer and sugary energy bar must go). One of the most important parts of this cleanse is drinking plenty of water to flush out all of the toxins that have accumulated in your body! Each day you should drink a minimum of 10 cups of water and other liquids. Other approved liquids on the cleanse include metabolism-boosting lemon water and green tea; herbal teas; and juices like the Spicy Ginger Carrot Juice (page 55) and the Green Ginger Sunshine Juice (page 59).

The meal plan on pages 50 and 51 shows you what two weeks of clean green eating looks like. Feel free to mix and match based on your taste preferences and the foods you have at home. For example, if you want to make a double batch of the Anti-Inflammatory Smoothie so you can have it two days in a row, go for it. Or if you'd rather have a green juice for breakfast and the smoothie as your snack, you can switch up the order. These are just guidelines. I wanted to create a meal plan of plant-based recipes that contain the most nutrients and natural detoxifiers, and are the lowest in added sugars. Trust me, your body is going to absolutely love you for this!

If you find yourself eating out or away from home during your two-week cleanse, here are some basic guidelines for choosing a healthy meal that won't derail your progress.

WHAT TO EAT:

➤ Fresh greens and vegetables (organic when possible, unlimited!)

➤ Fresh fruits: limit to a piece a day

➤ Whole grains, cracked grains, and sprouted grains: limit to 1 cup or less per day

➤ Nuts and seeds: limit to ½ cup a day

➤ Beans and legumes

➤ Sea vegetables (be sure to check sodium content)

➤ Spices like turmeric, cayenne, ginger, cinnamon, fennel, and cumin

WHAT TO DRINK:

➤ Water: 10 cups a day

➤ Lemon water (see page 41)

➤ Green tea

➤ Fresh green juices: limit to 2 a day, low in sugar

➤ Herbal teas

➤ Unsweetened nut-, rice, and coconut milk: all nutmilks in moderation; all unsweetened

WHAT TO LIMIT/AVOID:

➤ Animal protein

➤ Dairy

➤ Added sugar: no soda or sugary drinks

➤ Alcohol

➤ Caffeine: coffee and green tea are OK in moderation, but no sweet creamer; try nutmilks in your coffee and tea if needed

➤ Artificial sweeteners (never, ever!)

➤ Added salt

➤ Processed and packaged foods, including protein or granola bars, bread, crackers, chips, and other junk food (remember, clean eating is about nourishing that body with real food)

➤ Fast food: don't even go there!

While You're Cleansing

A cleanse isn't just about the food you're putting in your body—it is an opportunity for a total reset—mind, body, and soul. Here are a few ways to support your cleansing efforts and gain the maximum results.

MOVE: Because this is not a fast and you're not drastically restricting your caloric intake, you should still have plenty of energy for exercise. I highly recommend getting your blood pumping and your body sweating daily while you are cleansing—it helps to speed the removal of toxins from your body, it supports your weight-loss efforts, and it just plain makes you feel good! Studies have shown that regular exercise can help alleviate depression, boost brain health, and even keep your immunity strong. Even as little as 30 minutes of movement a day can do your hot body good. You're already setting aside two weeks to take care of your precious body—30 minutes is nothing!

REST: While we're on the topic of counting minutes and hours . . . it is so important to give your body a break while you are cleansing and get 7 to 8 hours of sleep every night. That means lights out at a decent hour—no late nights at work, at home, or out with friends. Sleep is when your body repairs, detoxes, and recovers on a cellular level (and that includes skin cells, so it literally is beauty sleep!). Sleep can also help to relieve stress, boost energy, and improve cognitive performance. Lack of sleep has been linked to obesity, a weak immune system, and even heart disease and diabetes. Trust me, this is one healthy habit that is a pleasure to indulge in. Once you start to get more sleep on a regular basis, you will soon find yourself craving an early bedtime every night!

RELAX: Have you been reading all the buzz about meditation lately? Though this ancient practice for clearing the mind has been around forever, it seems to be finally getting its due. The benefits of a regular meditation practice are many, and include reduced stress and anxiety, a sharper mind, and an enhanced immune system.

While you're cleansing, make it a goal to meditate once a day. It can be for as little as five or ten minutes when you're starting out—whatever time you have is fine, just try to be consistent about meditating at the same time each day, and practice in the same space to establish a ritual. I love to meditate in the mornings when I wake up. I sit on the floor, place my hands on my knees (palms up to receive good energy, palms down to stay grounded), and breathe in and out deeply. For beginning meditators, there are plenty of resources from Deepak Chopra to a popular app called "Headspace," or even a local meditation course you can look up, but the main thing is to breathe deeply and focus on your breath while you allow your mind to clear. If a thought or worry creeps in, it's OK, just observe it and calmly let it go. For many people it helps to have a mantra to focus on. I like to internally say to myself: "Clear mind, no drama, beautiful day." Once you start making clean and clear mental space you'll find that you are able to not only be more mindful, but also happier and more creative.

ENJOY! : Just because you're cleansing doesn't mean you can't still have fun! It's probably not a great idea to meet up for happy hour while you're cleansing, but you can still meet up for a green juice, a tea, or a yoga or spin class together. Being part of a social group can give you a sense of community and help you feel more connected to others. Try this cleanse with a friend! I know that when I spend time with my girlfriends, I always feel better. Social activity is an instant pick-me-up that is healthy for your mind and your body. And it's free!

Clean Green Cleanse Meal Plan

OK, friends, here it is: two weeks of clean green eating. Remember, there are no hard-and-fast rules here, no calorie restrictions, no hunger pangs. Think of this as a way to nourish your body with an abundance of clean eating, not punish it with deprivation. Trust me, when you feed your body with the nutrition it craves, it will love you back!

Clean Green Cleanse: *Week One*

WEEK ONE	MONDAY	TUESDAY	WEDNESDAY	THURSDAY	FRIDAY	SATURDAY	SUNDAY
Clean Green Breakfast Smoothie	Chocolate-Banana Love Smoothie (page 65)	Coconut-Almond Green Smoothie (page 66)	Açai Beauty Smoothie (page 64)	Hawaiian Clean Green Smoothie (page 66)	The Anti-inflammatory Smoothie (page 68)	Pineapple Horchata Green Smoothie (page 62)	Chocolate-Banana Love Smoothie (page 65)
Cleansing Lunch	Clean Green Minestrone (page 123)	Baked potato with marinara sauce and kale	½ cup oatmeal with banana and peanut butter	Clean Green Minestrone (page 123)	Kale Quinoa Tabbouleh (page 100)	Large seaweed salad with green tea	Clean Green Barley Walnut Soup (page 126)
Refreshing Beverages (optional in addition to 10 cups of water a day!)	Lemon Water	Green Tea	Lemon Water	Ginger-Melon Juice (page 54)	Green Tea	Green Ginger Sunshine Juice (page 59)	Sweet Kale Lemonade (page 56)
Clean Green Dinner	Roasted Sweet Potato and Avocado Bowl with Carrot-Ginger Vinaigrette (page 190)	Curly Kale with Tahini Garlic Dressing (page 108)	Red Lentil Soup (page 125)	Clean Green Kale and Mushroom Frittata (page 92)	Sun-Dried Tomato and Tofu Farro Salad (page 166)	Lemon-Soy Edamame Barley Bowl (page 189)	Shaved Brussels Sprouts Salad (page 106)
Snacks (in moderation)				A handful of raw almonds, walnuts or cashews. Blueberries, an apple, or stone fruit like peaches or nectarines. Half an avocado with lemon and soy sauce. Fresh veggies with guacamole hummus (page 140).			
Bedtime Tea (optional, but perfect to curb cravings)				Chamomile, fennel seed, ginger, or lavender tea with honey, Yogi Calming tea, or Yogi Peach Detox tea.			

Clean Green Cleanse: *Week Two*

WEEK TWO	MONDAY	TUESDAY	WEDNESDAY	THURSDAY	FRIDAY	SATURDAY	SUNDAY
Clean Green Breakfast Smoothie	Hawaiian Clean Green Smoothie (page 66)	Pineapple Horchata Green Smoothie (page 62)	Anti-inflammatory Smoothie (page 68)	Coconut-Almond Green Smoothie (page 66)	Pineapple Horchata Green Smoothie (page 62)	Kale-Chocolate Protein Smoothie (page 68)	Chocolate-Banana Love Smoothie (page 65)
Cleansing Lunch	Bowl of fresh fruit with almond butter and flax seed meal	Clean Green Barley Walnut Soup (page 126)	Parsnip and Leek Detox Soup (page 122)	½ avocado smashed over whole-wheat toast and flax seed	Large seaweed salad with green tea	Kale Quinoa Tabbouleh (page 100)	Baked potato with marinara sauce and kale
Refreshing Beverages (optional in addition to 10 cups of water a day!)	Lemon Water	Green Tea	Spicy Ginger Carrot Juice (page 55)	Sweet Kale Lemonade (page 56)	Green Tea	Green Ginger Sunshine Juice (page 59)	Green Tea
Clean Green Dinner	Roasted Kabocha Squash and Quinoa Soup (page 131)	Avocado and Grape-fruit Salad (page 102)	Tofu Curry and Greens Salad (page 115)	Roasted Sweet Potato and Avocado Bowl with Carrot-Ginger Vinaigrette (page 190)	Macrobiotic Hijiki-Avocado Salad (page 116)	Avocado-Kale Caesar Salad (page 105)	Roasted Kabocha Squash Salad (page 174)
Snacks (in moderation)				1 cup of raw veggies with tahini or hummus, ½ cup of homemade granola (page 80), ¼ cup homemade roasted almonds or cashews (page 143). Blueberries or an apple.			
Bedtime Tea (optional, but perfect to curb cravings)				Chamomile, fennel seed, ginger, or lavender tea with honey, Yogi Calming tea, or Yogi Peach Detox tea.			

3

CLEAN GREEN CLEANSING JUICES AND SMOOTHIES

THE GREATEST WEALTH IS HEALTH.

—Virgil

CLEAN MOJITO JUICE

With fresh mint, cucumber, and melon, this spa-worthy juice is perfect for everyday detoxing. **Serves 2; yields 12 ounces**

1 large cucumber, unpeeled
¼ cup honeydew melon, sliced, rind removed
¼ cup fresh mint leaves
¼ lime, whole

Put all the ingredients into a high-powered juicer and juice. Serve immediately.

SPINACH-GINGER CLEANSER

Good morning, fresh ginger! Add some spice, as well as anti-inflammatory compounds, into your life with this clean green drink. It will start your day off with a kick for breakfast, and is also the perfect late-day pick-me-up.
Serves 2; yields 12 ounces

1 large cucumber, unpeeled
4 cups baby spinach
3 tablespoons fresh ginger
¼ cup honeydew melon, sliced, rind removed

Put all the ingredients into a high-powered juicer and juice. Serve immediately.

GINGER-MELON JUICE

This combination of ginger and melon is so simple, yet unexpected. It's light, sweet, and a little spicy . . . the perfect post-workout drink to help reduce inflammation after sweating it out! **Serves 1; yields 8 ounces**

¼ cup honeydew melon, sliced, rind removed

2 tablespoons fresh ginger

1 medium cucumber, unpeeled

Put all the ingredients into a high-powered juicer and juice. Serve immediately.

COCONUT-MANGO DREAM JUICE

The luscious combination of fresh coconut and mango will transport you straight to the tropics, while a healthy dose of greens and coconut water will keep you hydrated and energized all day long. **Serves 2; yields 11 ounces**

4 cups baby spinach

¼ cup fresh coconut pieces

¼ cup peeled and sliced mango

1 cup coconut water (no sugar added)

Put all the ingredients into a high-powered juicer and juice. Serve immediately.

SPICY GINGER CARROT JUICE

If you're a fan of carrot cake, this is going to be your new fave juice. I love making this cayenne-and-ginger-spiced blend first thing in the morning—it's like having a carrot muffin for breakfast, minus all of the calories, sugar, and carbs!

Serves 1; yields 7 ounces

6 carrots, peeled, ends removed

2 tablespoons fresh ginger

Dash of cayenne pepper

Put all the ingredients into a high-powered juicer and juice. Add the cayenne, and whisk to incorporate. Serve immediately.

SWEET KALE LEMONADE

Refreshing, cleansing, and delicious, this superfood-packed juice will have you feeling clean from the inside out. Who needs beauty creams and serums when you're getting all of that vitamin K, vitamin C, plus antioxidants in one tasty drink? **Serves 2; yields 18 ounces**

1½ large cucumbers, unpeeled
1 lemon, peeled
2 cups kale leaves, tough stems removed
2 cups baby spinach
¼ Fuji apple

Put all the ingredients into a high-powered juicer and juice. Serve immediately.

WATERMELON REFRESHER

Who needs processed sugar-water sports drinks when you can get natural electrolytes and hydration from melon, spinach, and cucumber? This light and refreshing combination is perfect post-workout or on a hot summer day. **Serves 2; yields 15 ounces**

3 cups baby spinach
1 cup watermelon, sliced, rind removed
2 tablespoons fresh ginger
1 medium cucumber, unpeeled

Put all the ingredients into a high-powered juicer and juice. Serve immediately.

Sweet Kale Lemonade

Clean Green Skin Detox

CLEAN GREEN
SKIN DETOX

Cucumbers, apple, lemon, and apple cider vinegar all work together to help calm and hydrate that beautiful complexion of yours. Whisk the apple cider vinegar in at the end to finish off this skin-glowing cocktail. **Serves 2; yields 12 ounces**

1 large cucumber, unpeeled
⅛ Fuji apple
½ lemon, peeled
2 tablespoons raw, unfiltered apple cider vinegar

Put the cucumber, apple, and lemon into a high-powered juicer and juice. Add the apple cider vinegar to the juice and whisk well to incorporate. Serve immediately.

GREEN GINGER
SUNSHINE JUICE

Waking up on those icky rainy days is never easy. Bring instant sunshine into your morning with this delicious, sunny juice combo. I promise you it will start your morning off on the sunnier side! **Serves 2; yields 13 ounces**

1 large cucumber, unpeeled
4 cups baby spinach
3 tablespoons fresh ginger
¼ cup fresh pineapple

Put all the ingredients into a high-powered juicer and juice. Serve immediately.

CUCUMBER ALOE
MELON JUICE

After a fabulous morning yoga session, or a run with the man, opt to juice this electrolyte-packed refresher. You'll be a fan of aloe's immunity-boosting powers and hydration, along with its nutritious bennies. Not just for cuts and scrapes, aloe is great for the inside of your body as well! Delish! **Serves 2; yields 18 ounces**

1½ large cucumbers, unpeeled
3 tablespoons peeled aloe vera leaves
¼ cup honeydew melon, sliced, rind removed
4 cups baby spinach
½ cup fresh mint leaves

Put all the ingredients into a high-powered juicer and juice. Serve immediately.

CLEAN GREEN JUICERS!: When selecting a juicer, get smart. Invest in a masticating, cold-pressed juicer, like a Hurom, Omega, or Norwalk juicer. Masticating juicers crush juice with little or no heat, giving you the full benefits of fresh juicing! Happy crushing!

WATERMELON-BASIL
JUICE

If you're a big fan of watermelon and basil salads, you're going to love this clean, green juice. Be sure to inhale that fresh, fragrant basil as you juice, which is thought to relax and calm the mind! **Serves 2; yields 15 ounces**

1½ large cucumbers, unpeeled
¼ cup fresh basil leaves
½ cup watermelon, sliced, rind removed

Put all the ingredients into a high-powered juicer and juice. Serve immediately.

Cucumber Aloe Melon Juice

PINEAPPLE HORCHATA
GREEN SMOOTHIE

Growing up in sunny San Diego, we had no shortage of a great *horchata*—a milky Latin American drink that can be made from seeds, rice, nuts, or dairy. This delicious and good-for-you version uses a nondairy coconut milk drink and bananas to create a smooth, creamy texture. Vanilla, cinnamon, and pineapple add delicious sweetness without any added sugar! **Serves 2; yields 20 ounces**

1 frozen banana (or swap for 1 avocado to reduce sugar)
¼ cup fresh pineapple
2 tablespoons unsweetened shredded coconut
2 cups baby spinach
1 teaspoon ground cinnamon
½ teaspoon organic vanilla extract
1 cup unsweetened coconut milk drink

Combine all the ingredients in a blender and blend until smooth. Serve immediately.

CLEAN GREEN JUICE TIP!: This smoothie contains natural sugars, so be sure to moderate your sugar consumption and split this smoothie with your loved ones. Trust me, they will love you for it!

THE AÇAI BEAUTY SMOOTHIE

This berry-packed açai smoothie is a natural immunity booster, with a healthy dose of antioxidants. I like to add a scoop of plant-based protein to this smoothie for a filling breakfast or lunch on the go, or even a post-workout recovery drink.

Serves 2; yields 20 ounces

2 frozen açai smoothie packs (1 cup frozen açai; look for frozen Sambazon packets)

¼ frozen banana (or swap for ½ avocado to reduce sugar)

¼ cup frozen blueberries

1½ cups baby spinach

1 tablespoon fresh lemon juice

1 cup unsweetened coconut milk drink

1 scoop pea protein powder (optional)

Combine all the ingredients in a blender and blend until smooth. Serve immediately.

CLEAN GREEN SMOOTHIE TIP: Why all the frozen berries!? Well, frozen berries blend up smooth and beautifully compared to fresh berries. Not to worry, these berries are picked at peak season before packaging, so they are still packed with vitamin C, antioxidants, and major health benefits.

AÇAI BANANA PROTEIN SMOOTHIE

Almond butter plus frozen bananas plus açai?! You can thank me later. In the meantime, you can thank yourself for eating all of these antioxidants—you'll be looking 10 years younger in no time, gorgeous. **Serves 2; yields 16 ounces**

1 frozen banana (or swap for 1 avocado to reduce sugar)

1 frozen packet açai (I recommend the Sambazon brand)

1 cup baby spinach

2 tablespoons unsweetened almond butter

1 scoop pea protein powder
1 cup unsweetened almond milk drink

Combine all the ingredients in a blender and blend until smooth. Serve immediately.

CHOCOLATE-BANANA LOVE SMOOTHIE

After all these years of recipe development and cookbooks, how could I not have had a chocolate banana love drink!? Two of my favorites, in one. Well, here you are; a smoothie with the perfect balance of flavors, plus super-healthy greens, spinach, and spirulina. Get ready to clean green banana chocolate karate chop in the a.m.! **Serves 2; yields 18 ounces**

2 bananas, frozen
2 tablespoons unsweetened cocoa powder
1 cup unsweetened coconut almond milk blend (add ¼ to ½ cup more, as desired)
1 cup baby spinach
1 teaspoon spirulina powder

Combine all the ingredients in a blender and blend until smooth. Serve immediately.

CLEAN GREEN TIP: For the quick-and-simple and smooth, ice cream-like smoothies, I recommend using frozen bananas exclusively. Be sure to freeze your bananas ahead of time! Place your unpeeled, ripe bananas into a resealable freezer bag. Make sure all of the air is out of the bag, seal well, and place into the freezer. Freeze the bananas for at least 5 hours, and break apart as needed when ready to use.

COCONUT-ALMOND
GREEN SMOOTHIE

Creamy, delectable almond butter is full of vitamin E and protein—and when paired with shredded coconut, frozen bananas, and almond milk, this creamy, delicious smoothie tastes more like a thick, dreamy green milkshake! **Serves 2; yields 16 ounces**

2 tablespoons unsweetened almond butter
2 tablespoons unsweetened shredded coconut
1 cup baby spinach
1 teaspoon spirulina powder
1 frozen banana (or swap for 1 avocado to reduce sugar)
¾ cup unsweetened almond milk
1 teaspoon organic vanilla extract

Combine all the ingredients in a blender and blend until smooth. Serve immediately.

THE HAWAIIAN CLEAN
GREEN SMOOTHIE

I go to my beloved Hawaii once a year—it is one of my favorite places on earth. This smoothie, made with coconut, mango, and banana, reminds me of some of my favorite fresh island flavors. Whenever possible, look for spirulina powder that is harvested in Hawaii! Aloha! **Serves 1; yields 10 ounces**

¼ cup frozen mango chunks
¼ frozen banana
2 tablespoons fresh coconut pieces (can sub with unsweetened shredded coconut)
1 cup baby spinach
¾ cup coconut water
1 teaspoon spirulina powder

Combine all the ingredients in a blender and blend until smooth. Serve immediately.

Coconut-Almond Green Smoothie

KALE-CHOCOLATE PROTEIN SMOOTHIE

Have some leftover fresh kale from dinner last night? Well, guess what—it's breakfast this morning! Grab a handful and toss it in with protein-rich walnuts, inflammation-fighting cinnamon, and more for a super-power-packed breakfast smoothie. **Serves 2; yields 18 ounces**

1 frozen banana (or swap for 1 avocado to reduce sugar)
¼ cup raw walnuts
¾ cup kale, stems removed, chopped
1 scoop pea protein powder (optional)
½ teaspoon spirulina powder
2 tablespoons unsweetened cocoa powder
¼ teaspoon ground cinnamon
1 cup unsweetened almond milk

Combine all the ingredients in a blender and blend until smooth. Serve immediately.

THE ANTI-INFLAMMATORY SMOOTHIE

My boyfriend and I created this delish smoothie after he needed an anti-inflammation kick! We loved the natural, positively packed anti-inflammatory powers from the blueberries, blackberries, and walnuts—it tastes like a berry milkshake! Try it out with a loved one, too, and share the clean green love!

Serves 3; yields 30 ounces

1 frozen banana (or swap for 1 avocado to reduce sugar)
¾ cup frozen blueberries
¾ frozen blackberries
1½ cups unsweetened almond milk
1 teaspoon bee pollen
¼ cup raw walnuts
1 cup baby spinach
1 teaspoon spirulina powder (optional)

Combine all the ingredients in a blender and blend until smooth. Serve immediately.

The Anti-Inflammatory Smoothie

4

GREEN AND GORGEOUS
BREAKFASTS AND BRUNCHES

YOU DO NOT NEED TO LIKE THEM. SO YOU SAY.
TRY THEM! TRY THEM! AND YOU MAY.

—DR. SEUSS, *Green Eggs and Ham*

CREAMY COCONUT OATMEAL

Who doesn't love a hot bowl of oatmeal in the morning? Not only are oats inexpensive and easy to cook, they are also packed with fiber and cholesterol-lowering benefits. This delicious breakfast bowl will keep you fueled all morning long. **Serves 4**

2 cups unsweetened coconut milk drink

1 cup water

$\frac{1}{8}$ teaspoon sea salt

$2\frac{1}{2}$ cups organic rolled oats

1 cup fresh papaya slices (or mango)

2 tablespoons toasted, unsweetened, shredded coconut

1 tablespoon manuka honey (optional)

Bring the coconut milk drink, water, and salt to a boil in a medium saucepan over high heat. Add the oats and cook, stirring, for 6 to 8 minutes. Cover, turn off heat, and let it absorb for 5 minutes.

Spoon the oatmeal into two bowls, then top with papaya (or mango) slices, toasted coconut, and honey, if using. Mix with a spoon and enjoy!

GREEN GRANOLA BARS

People think of granola bars as healthy, but most of them are packed with refined sugar, preservatives, and other processed junk. It's easy to make your own at home—and cost-effective, too! I love to make a batch of these before a trip with friends so we all have a go-to snack. You can also package them up with parchment paper and twine for a pretty and healthy gift! **Yields 12 bars**

Coconut oil, or olive oil cooking spray, for the baking sheet

DRY INGREDIENTS

2 cups organic rolled oats

¾ cup raw sliced almonds

½ cup raw pepitas

½ cup raw sunflower seeds

½ cup unsweetened shredded coconut

¼ cup toasted sesame seeds

2 tablespoons flaxseed meal

1 cup dried cherries

1 teaspoon spirulina powder (optional)

WET INGREDIENTS

½ cup brown rice syrup

¾ cup unsweetened almond butter

2 teaspoons organic vanilla extract

1 tablespoon coconut oil

½ teaspoon sea salt

Preheat the oven to 350°F. Line a baking sheet with aluminum foil and coat lightly with coconut oil or olive oil cooking spray. Spray or butter a 9 x 13-inch baking dish, line it with parchment paper or aluminum foil, and set aside.

Spread out the oats, almonds, pepitas, sunflower seeds, and shredded coconut on the prepared baking sheet and roast in the oven for 8 to 10 minutes.

In the meantime, in a large saucepan over low heat, combine the brown rice syrup, almond butter, vanilla, coconut oil, and salt and cook, stirring, until heated through and combined well using a spatula.

Once the granola mixture has toasted, remove it from the oven, add the toasted sesame seeds, flaxseed meal, dried cherries, and spirulina powder, if using, and toss to evenly combine. Using the foil as an aid, transfer the granola mixture into the large saucepan with the wet mixture. Mix well with a spatula to coat evenly.

Once the mixture is well combined and slightly cool, pour the granola into the prepared baking dish and press it down firmly, to evenly distribute it in the dish. Let cool for at least an hour, or overnight.

Cut into squares and store in an airtight container for up to a week.

THE ULTIMATE KALE
BREAKFAST BURRITO

This breakfast burrito is absolute delicious madness. The combination of scrambled eggs, mushrooms, kale, cheese, avocado, and sriracha is a pretty amazing way to start off a lazy Saturday or Sunday. If you make these for a large brunch, you'd better double the recipe—your friends will keep coming back for more! **Serves 4**

2 tablespoons extra-virgin olive oil

½ yellow onion, finely chopped

2 cups cremini mushrooms, thinly sliced

1 cup lacinato kale, tough ribs removed, finely chopped

6 eggs

¼ teaspoon sea salt

¼ teaspoon freshly ground black pepper

1 teaspoon granulated garlic powder

2 tablespoons Pecorino Romano cheese, grated, plus more for topping (optional)

4 large whole-wheat tortillas, warmed through on a stove top

TOPPINGS

1 ripe avocado, thinly sliced

¼ cup finely shredded Pecorino Romano or Manchego cheese (optional)

Sriracha sauce (optional)

In a large sauté pan, warm the olive oil over medium-low heat. Add the chopped onion and sauté for 5 minutes, or until translucent. Add the sliced mushrooms and sauté for an additional 3 minutes, or until the liquid from the mushrooms has cooked off. Reduce the heat to low and add the kale. Cook until the kale has wilted slightly. Transfer the mushroom-kale mixture to a small bowl and set aside to cool.

In a medium bowl, using a fork, whisk together the eggs, salt, pepper, garlic powder, and cheese, if using. Pour the egg mixture into the sauté pan over low heat. Using a spatula, scramble the eggs just until set; they should still be slightly undercooked. Then fold in the mushroom-kale mixture.

Lay out the warmed-through tortillas and evenly spread half of the scrambled egg mixture onto each. Sprinkle lightly with additional cheese, if using. Fold over one side and roll into a burrito shape. Repeat with the remaining tortillas. Top with avocado slices and sriracha sauce, if desired.

BIRCHER MUESLI

V

I am totally obsessed with the overnight muesli trend. The prep (inspired by my sweet Dean and Karen, direct from Switzerland!) is super simple—just soak the oats the night before and add fresh fruit and whatever toppings you want in the morning. This recipe is unreal—I have tested it many times for your enjoyment (and my tasting!). *Start this recipe the night before!* **Serves 4**

1¾ cups organic rolled oats
1 cup organic orange juice or apple juice (try making it fresh in your juicer!)
¼ cup unsweetened shredded coconut
¼ cup unsweetened dried cranberries
½ cup sliced, raw almonds
½ cup raw pepitas
1 cup Greek yogurt (I prefer low-fat 2 percent)
1 Fuji, Honeycrisp, or Gala apple, unpeeled, halved, and cut into ¾-inch cubes
½ teaspoon freshly grated nutmeg (optional)

In a medium airtight container, combine the oats and juice, place in the fridge, and allow the oats to soak overnight.

In the morning, pour the oats into a bowl. Add the shredded coconut, cranberries, almonds, and pepitas to the bowl and combine with the oats. Fold in the yogurt and the cubed apple. Top with grated nutmeg, if desired. Serve cold, or place into the fridge for up to 4 days.

CLEAN GREEN TIP: If you love fresh berries or banana slices, swap out the apple for other delish fruit. Or, if you prefer walnuts or sunflower seeds, use those in place of almonds. Or use dried cherries in place of cranberries. Be creative and fabulous!

CINNAMON-SPICED GRANOLA

This delicious, make-ahead recipe is perfect to bake up on a Sunday evening to have on hand all week long. I like to store it in mason jars that I can take with me to work. Enjoy it paired with a sprinkle of fresh fruit, almond milk, or Greek yogurt. It's important to add the spirulina powder *after* the granola is removed from the oven so that you get the maximum nutritional benefit from this superfood booster. **Serves 6; yields 4 cups**

Coconut oil or olive oil cooking spray, for the baking sheet
2 cups organic rolled oats
1 cup whole, raw almonds
½ cup whole, raw pepitas
2 tablespoons whole, raw flaxseeds
3 tablespoons unrefined coconut oil
3 tablespoons manuka or raw honey
2 tablespoons unsweetened shredded coconut
1 teaspoon ground cinnamon
1 teaspoon freshly grated nutmeg
1 teaspoon ginger powder
½ teaspoon sea salt
¼ cup dried cranberries
1 teaspoon spirulina powder (optional)

Preheat the oven to 325°F. Line a baking sheet with aluminum foil and coat it with coconut oil or olive oil cooking spray. Spread out the oats, almonds, pepitas, and flaxseeds on the prepared baking sheet, place on the middle rack, and toast for 10 minutes.

Meanwhile, in a large bowl, whisk together the 3 tablespoons coconut oil, honey, unsweetened coconut, cinnamon, nutmeg, ginger, and salt until combined.

When the oat mixture is toasted, remove it from the oven and let cool slightly. Combine the oat mixture with the liquid mixture in the bowl, and toss to coat. Reserve the baking sheet. Spread the oat mixture evenly over the baking sheet. Bake for about 15 minutes on the middle rack, or until golden brown and crisp, keeping an eye on the granola, as all ovens vary in temperatures. Set aside.

Once the granola has cooled slightly, stir in the cranberries and spirulina powder, if using. Let the granola cool completely for at least 1 hour to fully crisp! Store in an airtight container for up to 2 weeks. Perfect for a delicious snack to go!

CHOCOLATE CHIP–BANANA PANCAKES

If you love the combination of bananas and chocolate as much as I do, you will love these fluffy, delightful, and clean green pancakes! With eggs, spirulina powder, and mashed banana, you can't go wrong with this decadent breakfast that also happens to be gluten-free. The secret to achieving perfect fluffiness is finishing off these pancakes in the oven! **Serves 4 to 6; yields about 12 pancakes using ¼ cup batter per pancake**

DRY INGREDIENTS

1½ cups gluten-free flour (look for delicious gluten-free blends with garbanzo bean flour)
1 teaspoon baking soda
¼ teaspoon sea salt
1 tablespoon spirulina powder (optional)

WET INGREDIENTS

3 large eggs
1 tablespoon maple syrup or brown rice syrup
1 teaspoon organic vanilla extract
½ cup unsweetened almond milk
1 ripe banana, mashed with a fork

Coconut oil or olive oil cooking spray, for the pan
¼ cup dark chocolate chips (60 percent cacao or more)
Pure maple syrup, for topping

Preheat the oven to 350°F. Line two baking sheets with aluminum foil.

In a large bowl, whisk together the flour, baking soda, salt, and spirulina powder, if using. In a medium bowl, whisk together the eggs, maple syrup or brown rice syrup, vanilla, and almond milk, then gently fold in the mashed banana. Using a rubber spatula, add the mixture to the dry ingredients in the large bowl and stir gently just until combined.

Heat a large nonstick skillet over medium heat. Coat the pan with coconut oil or olive oil cooking spray. Ladle in the batter, using ¼ cup for each pancake, sprinkle with chocolate chips, and cook the pancakes until the outer edges firm up, the pancakes bubble slightly, and the bottoms are golden brown, about 1 minute. Flip and cook the opposite sides until golden brown, 1 more minute.

Transfer the pancakes to the lined baking sheets and set aside. Continue cooking the remaining batter, transferring the pancakes to the baking sheets once they're browned. (If you only have one baking sheet, and run out of space, stack the pancakes, but for the fluffiest pancakes, use two baking sheets.) Pop the baking sheets in the oven and cook the pancakes for an additional 5 minutes. Plate and serve with maple syrup or other toppings of your choice, and remember to keep sugar to a minimum to stay clean!

BLUEBERRY BLISS
FLAX ZUCCHINI BREAD

This delicious loaf is naturally moist and filling, with that zucchini bread texture you crave—you would never know it's vegan and gluten-free! Packed with omega-3s plus plenty of fiber and protein from the flaxseed, one slice of this makes a perfect breakfast-on-the-go. **Yields one 8-inch loaf**

½ cup flaxseed meal
⅓ cup almond meal
1¼ cups gluten-free flour
¼ teaspoon sea salt
½ teaspoon ground cinnamon
½ teaspoon freshly grated nutmeg
⅓ cup coconut sugar OR ⅓ cup granulated sugar
1 teaspoon organic vanilla extract
⅔ cup water
1 tablespoons raw, unfiltered apple cider vinegar
1 teaspoon baking soda
1 small green zucchini, finely grated (about ¾ cups)
1¼ cups frozen blueberries, divided
Confectioners' sugar, for dusting (optional)

Preheat the oven to 350°F. Line a 8 x 4-inch loaf pan with parchment paper and set aside.

In a large bowl, whisk together the flaxseed meal, almond meal, flour, salt, cinnamon, nutmeg, coconut sugar (or sugar), and vanilla. Slowly add the water and stir to combine.

In a small bowl, toss 1 cup of blueberries with a little flour to coat; this will prevent them from sinking in the batter. In a separate small bowl, combine the vinegar and baking soda, allow the mixture to fizz, then add to the mixture in the large bowl. Gently fold in the zucchini, followed by 1 cup of the blueberries and mix just to incorporate; do not overmix!

Carefully pour the batter into the prepared loaf pan, spreading the top out evenly with a spatula. Top with the remaining ¼ cup unfloured blueberries.

Bake the bread for about 55 minutes, or until golden brown on top. Let the loaf cool in the pan completely and dust the top with confectioners' sugar, if desired.

CLEAN GREEN TIPS: For the best results and the most even distribution of zucchini in your bread, use the fine (smallest) setting on your grater, or even a Microplane, when grating the zucchini. And when baking with blueberries, use frozen wild blueberries for the best results. They are smaller and easier to distribute evenly in baking loaves and cakes!

COCONUT-DATE SCONES

Beautiful, handmade, delicious scones are, believe it or not, a super-simple recipe for any beginner. I love the natural sweetness the dates add to these morning treats, and even better, I love that dates are packed with fiber, potassium, vitamin B$_6$, and magnesium. Bake these up on Saturday or Sunday morning and enjoy all week—if they last in your house that long! **Yields 8 to 12 scones**

Coconut oil or olive oil cooking spray, for the baking sheet
2 cups gluten-free flour, plus extra for rolling the dough
½ cup unsweetened shredded coconut; reserve 2 tablespoons for topping
2 teaspoons baking soda
¼ teaspoon sea salt
4 tablespoons (½ stick) cold unsalted butter, cut into small pieces
1 tablespoon fresh lemon juice
1 large whole egg
1 large egg yolk, beaten, for egg wash
¼ cup unsweetened organic applesauce
¼ cup brown rice syrup
¾ cup dried dates, pitted and roughly chopped
2 tablespoons turbinado sugar (optional)

Preheat the oven to 350°F. Line a baking sheet with aluminum foil and coat with coconut oil or olive oil cooking spray.

In a large bowl, mix together the flour, 6 tablespoons of the unsweetened shredded coconut, the baking soda, and sea salt. Cut in the butter, or rub it in with your fingers, until the mixture has a coarse, mealy texture.

In a separate large bowl, whisk together the lemon juice, whole egg, applesauce, and brown rice syrup. Combine the wet ingredients with the dry ingredients and mix carefully just until incorporated. Gently fold the chopped dates into the mixture, and toss in a bit of flour, as needed, to prevent your hands from sticking.

Turn out the dough onto a floured work surface, and gently knead dough just to incorporate the flour. Mold the dough into a 2-inch-thick round disk. Cut into 8 to 12 wedges (like a pie), depending on the size of scone you'd like.

Transfer the scones to the prepared baking sheet. Brush with the egg wash, and sprinkle with the reserved 2 tablespoons shredded coconut and the turbinado sugar, if desired. Bake on the middle rack until golden brown and cooked through, 12 to 14 minutes.

CLEAN GREEN TIP: Gently knead dough just to incorporate the flour and to achieve a soft dough. When baking breads (anything with added yeast), you do want to be sure to knead well to form strong gluten strands and allow your dough to rest.

MATCHA GREEN TEA CREPES

My great Auntie Takuko took me all over southern Japan, exploring the beauty, culture, and deliciousness of traditional preparations of matcha tea. This matcha crepe recipe is a delightful way to wake up in the morning and can double as an elegant and easy-to-whip-up dessert paired with fresh berries and a sprinkle of cinnamon! **Serves 4; yields 8 crepes**

WET INGREDIENTS

1 cup unsweetened almond milk
2 tablespoons maple syrup or brown rice syrup
1 large egg
1 teaspoon organic vanilla extract

DRY INGREDIENTS

1 cup gluten-free flour
1 tablespoon high-quality matcha powder
¼ teaspoon sea salt
Coconut oil or olive oil cooking spray, for the skillet

TOPPING OPTIONS

Greek yogurt
Fresh berries
Grade A maple syrup
Raw nuts
Unsweetened coconut flakes
Banana slices
Chocolate-hazelnut spread, in moderation
A dusting of matcha powder

In a medium bowl, whisk together the almond milk, maple syrup or brown rice syrup, egg, and vanilla until well combined. In a large bowl, whisk together the flour, matcha powder, and sea salt, then slowly incorporate into the wet ingredients. Continue to whisk until the batter is smooth. (The batter can be made the night before and refrigerated.)

Place a medium nonstick skillet over medium heat. Lightly coat the skillet with cooking spray. Ladle about ¼ cup of batter into the skillet. Using the back of the ladle, and working in a circular motion, spread the batter out into an even, paper-thin layer to cover the bottom of the skillet, tilting the skillet as needed. Cook the crepe until dry around the edges and golden brown, about 1 minute, then, using a rubber spatula, lift and flip the crepe. Cook the opposite side until golden brown, about another 30 seconds. Transfer the crepe to a large plate. Repeat making crepes with the remaining batter.

To serve, place a crepe on a clean work surface and top with the toppings of your choice. Fold the crepe in half, then in half again to make a triangle-wedge shape. Place the crepe on your serving plates and repeat with the remaining crepes (I like to serve 2 crepes per person). Top off with any additional favorites of yours—just be mindful of excess calories and sugar!

CLEAN GREEN TIP: Look to purchase high-quality true Japanese matcha powder. A great brand found in the United States is Matcha LOVE by Ito En. If you travel to Japan, pick up a real, traditional tin, and a matcha brush to bring home! Matcha can be stored in a cool, dry place for up to one year.

CAST-IRON SHAKSHUKA/CLEAN GREEN TOMATO AND EGGS OVER TOAST

This gorgeous, one-pan recipe was inspired by my talented and humble friend, Chef Marco Canora. The guy just knows how to achieve deep, rich flavors using real, fresh ingredients. You'll notice the egg whites are cooked separately from the yolks, a clever idea to thicken up the tomato sauce quickly. The runny yolks are just as aesthetically pleasing as they are delicious over whole-wheat toast and avocados. **Serves 4**

2 tablespoons extra-virgin olive oil

1 large yellow onion, finely chopped

2 garlic cloves, finely minced

One 28-ounce can whole plum or crushed tomatoes
    (if using whole, crush with your hands directly over the pan)

1 tablespoon dried oregano

1 teaspoon smoked paprika

¼ teaspoon sea salt

1 cup finely chopped lacinato kale leaves

6 large eggs, separated

4 slices whole-wheat or gluten-free bread, toasted

2 tablespoons fresh basil leaves, chiffonade, cut into thin ribbons

2 tablespoons fresh oregano leaves

1 ripe avocado, thinly sliced

In a large cast-iron skillet or sauté pan, warm the olive oil over medium heat. Add the chopped onion and sauté until soft and fragrant, about 8 minutes. Add the minced garlic and sauté for another 2 to 3 minutes.

Add the tomatoes to the skillet and cook on medium heat for 15 to 20 minutes, stirring occasionally. Add the dried oregano, smoked paprika, and salt to taste. Stir in the finely chopped kale and gently fold in the egg whites. Allow the egg whites to coagulate into the tomato sauce; reduce the heat to medium-low.

When the tomato sauce is thick and fragrant, begin to add your egg yolks to the top. Using the back of a spoon, gently create a little well for each yolk, and place the 6 yolks evenly across the top of the tomato mixture. Cook uncovered until the yolks are slightly set, but still a bit runny, about 8 minutes. Top with fresh basil leaves and oregano.

Place a trivet or pot holder directly on your dining table. Carefully remove the skillet from the heat, place on the trivet or pot holder along with a serving spoon. To plate, top a slice of whole-wheat toast with a spoonful of the tomato mixture and a few slices of avocado and prepare to go to heaven!

CLEAN GREEN KALE
AND MUSHROOM FRITTATA

A frittata may be the easiest way to make a clean, cheap, quick, and easy brunch recipe! Whip up this frittata the next time you have overnight guests. The great thing about making frittatas is that they go in the oven for 30 minutes, giving you time to set the table, do your makeup, throw together a fruit salad, or just hang and have a cup of joe with your fabulous guests! **Serves 6 to 8**

Coconut oil or olive oil cooking spray, for the pie plate
1 tablespoon extra-virgin olive oil
½ yellow onion, finely chopped
2 cups thinly sliced cremini or button mushrooms
6 large eggs, beaten
½ teaspoon sea salt
1 teaspoon granulated garlic powder
1 tablespoon flaxseed meal
1 to 2 tablespoons grated Pecorino Romano cheese, plus more for topping (optional)
½ teaspoon spirulina powder (optional)
1 cup finely chopped lacinato kale leaves
Fresh basil (optional)
Sriracha sauce (optional)

Preheat the oven to 350°F. Lightly coat an 8-inch round pie plate with coconut oil or olive oil cooking spray.

In a medium sauté pan, warm the olive oil over medium-low heat. Add the chopped onion and sauté until fragrant, about 8 minutes. Add the mushrooms and sauté until just softened, about 4 minutes. Reduce the heat to low and cook until the veggies are soft and the moisture has evaporated. Remove the pan from the heat and transfer the mixture to a small bowl to cool.

In a medium bowl, using a fork, whisk together the eggs, salt, garlic powder, flaxseed meal, cheese, and spirulina, if using. Fold in the finely chopped kale. Gently add the cooled onion-mushroom mixture and stir to combine. Pour the frittata mixture into the prepared pie plate and place on the middle rack of the oven. Bake for 30 to 35 minutes.

Check the frittata for doneness; the eggs should be set. Remove from the oven. Allow to cool for a few minutes, then cut into 6 to 8 pie-slice servings. Top with the additional cheese or torn fresh basil leaves, if desired. I like to serve this with sriracha sauce for a little extra kick.

CHOCOLATE-ALMOND BUTTER CHIA PUDDING

This chia seed pudding will take you minutes to whip up and will solidify in your fridge in just an hour (it gets even thicker and richer if chilled overnight). Chia seed pudding is a fabulous breakfast, brunch, snack, or dessert option, packed with protein and fiber. It's delicious topped with fresh banana slices or berries. Feel free to mix it up any way you like! **Serves 4**

1 tablespoon grade A maple syrup
3 tablespoons unsweetened almond butter
1 cup unsweetened almond milk
1 cup canned light coconut milk
½ cup chia seeds
2 tablespoons mini semi-sweet chocolate chips or carob, divided

Put the maple syrup and almond butter in a large bowl and whisk well to combine. Slowly stream in the almond milk and coconut milk and whisk to incorporate. Fold in the chia seeds and 1 tablespoon of the mini–chocolate chips (look for 60 percent cacao or higher).

Carefully pour the mixture into 4 to 6 sealable mason jars and chill in the refrigerator for at least 2 hours and up to overnight to set. (Chia seeds will absorb liquid, thicken, and expand to naturally create a creamy pudding-like texture.)

Serve chilled with the remaining mini–chocolate chips sprinkled on top.

GREEK YOGURT AND AMARANTH BERRY PORRIDGE

Strained yogurt may be the creamiest and most delightful treat nature has ever offered. Greek or Skyr, with few ingredients and minimal processing, its flavor is clean and rich, naturally. Add in your new favorite breakfast grain, amaranth, plus antioxidant-packed berries, and you've got yourself a slammin' treat for breakfast. **Serves 3**

2 cups water
1 cup unsweetened coconut milk drink or almond milk,
    plus more for pouring
1 cup uncooked amaranth
¼ teaspoon sea salt

TOPPINGS
3 tablespoons unsweetened almond butter
3 tablespoons Greek yogurt or Skyr Icelandic strained yogurt
3 teaspoons grade A honey, local, if possible (optional)
1 cup fresh berries (blueberries, blackberries, raspberries, or sliced strawberries)

In a medium saucepan, bring the water and coconut milk drink or almond milk to a boil. When the mixture boils, pour in the amaranth, reduce to a light simmer, stir in the sea salt, and cook for about 20 minutes, stirring occasionally, or until the mixture reaches a porridge-like consistency.

When the amaranth is cooked through, divide it equally among three breakfast bowls. Top each bowl with 1 tablespoon of almond butter and yogurt and 1 teaspoon honey, if using. Finish off each bowl with some berries and almond/coconut milk drink, if desired. Take your Instagram photo, mix, and eat!

CAROB SPIRULINA POWER BARS

I started to become a bit obsessed with these bars while traveling all over the country on a book tour. Make a batch ahead of time and pack them up before you travel! This nutrient-packed snack has the perfect level of crunch, with nuts and seeds, plus crisp brown rice cereal. Carob power adds a chocolatey flavor and extra fiber! Enjoy! **Yields twenty-four 2 x 2-inch squares or 12 bars**

DRY INGREDIENTS
¼ cup dried apricots
2 tablespoons spirulina powder
1 cup carob powder
⅛ teaspoon sea salt
½ cup whole, raw flaxseeds
1 cup whole, raw pepitas
1 cup whole, raw sunflower seeds
1½ cups crispy brown rice cereal or crisp rice cereal

WET INGREDIENTS
¾ cup grade A honey
1 cup unsweetened almond butter

Line an 8 x 8-inch baking pan or 9 x 13-inch baking pan with parchment paper.

Add the dried apricots to a large food processor and pulse to create a paste. Remove the paste from the food processor and set aside.

In a large heatproof bowl, toss together the spirulina powder, carob powder, and sea salt, and combine well, using your hands if needed.

In a large stockpot over low heat, melt the honey, almond butter, and reserved apricot paste and mix well with a rubber spatula for 2 to 3 minutes to incorporate. Make sure the mixture is smooth and free of any lumps.

Carefully remove the pot from the heat and fold in the flaxseeds, pepitas, sunflower seeds, and crispy rice cereal and mix well to combine and coat. Using a spatula, carefully transfer the seed mixture to the dry mixture and fold to combine. Be careful not to crush the crisp rice!

When the bar mixture is well combined, use a rubber spatula to gently press the mixture into the prepared baking pan, flattening to make ¾- to 1-inch bars. Allow the mixture to cool and harden. Cut into small squares or rectangles and enjoy as a super-power snack!

5

CLEAN GREEN
SALADS

YOUR BODY IS PRECIOUS. IT IS YOUR VEHICLE FOR AWAKENING.
TREAT IT WITH CARE.

— Buddha

KALE QUINOA TABBOULEH

If you love the Middle Eastern flavor combination of mint, cucumber, and lemon juice, you'll find this simple salad absolutely delicious. Pair with some flatbread and fresh tomato slices and you've got a perfect clean green, nutritionally packed lunch. **Serves 6**

2 cups uncooked quinoa

3½ cups water

2 cups lacinato kale, tough ribs removed,
   finely chopped

1 small cucumber, unpeeled, cut into small cubes

¼ cup chopped fresh mint leaves

¼ red onion, finely chopped

LEMON OLIVE OIL DRESSING

¼ cup plus 1 tablespoon fresh lemon juice

1 teaspoon finely grated lemon zest

1½ teaspoons granulated garlic powder

2 tablespoons reduced-sodium tamari soy sauce

2 tablespoons extra-virgin olive oil

Place the quinoa in a fine-mesh strainer and rinse well with cold water.

In a medium saucepan, combine the quinoa and water and bring to a boil over medium-high heat. Reduce the heat to medium and cook, uncovered, until all of the water has been absorbed and the quinoa is fluffy, about 15 minutes. Set aside to cool.

Prep the remaining salad ingredients.

In a large bowl, whisk together the lemon juice, lemon zest, garlic powder, tamari soy sauce, and olive oil. Add the chopped kale, cucumber, mint, and red onion to the bowl and toss well to coat with the dressing. Add the cooled quinoa and mix all the ingredients together. Serve chilled or at room temperature.

ROTISSERIE CHICKEN AND CHOPPED KALE SALAD WITH CREAMY SMOKED PAPRIKA VINAIGRETTE

This recipe is perfect for any leftover protein—chicken, turkey, tofu, or even jackfruit. But it's the Creamy Smoked Paprika Vinaigrette that really makes this salad shine! Feel free to swap out goat cheese for another cheese if you prefer—freshly grated Parmesan or crumbles of blue cheese or even a vegan cheese would all be delicious. **Serves 4**

4 cups lacinato kale leaves, tough ribs removed,
    finely chopped into bite-size pieces
2 cups leftover rotisserie chicken, chopped
2 plum tomatoes, finely diced
1 ear of corn, grilled and shaved
1 ripe avocado, pitted and cut into cubes
2 tablespoons crumbled goat cheese (chèvre) (optional)
2 tablespoons fresh cilantro leaves, chopped (optional)

CREAMY SMOKED PAPRIKA VINAIGRETTE

2 tablespoons olive oil mayonnaise
1 tablespoon extra-virgin olive oil
3 tablespoons fresh lemon juice
1 teaspoon smoked paprika
¼ teaspoon sea salt

Prep all the ingredients for the salad.

In a large bowl, whisk together the dressing: the olive oil mayonnaise, lemon juice, smoked paprika, and sea salt Add the chopped kale, chicken, tomatoes, corn, and avocado to the bowl and toss to combine with the vinaigrette. Finish the salad with the crumbled goat cheese and fresh cilantro, if desired.

AVOCADO AND GRAPEFRUIT SALAD

Avocados, again? Of course!—they are the most perfect fruit ever, in my California-girl opinion! I decided to cut the richness and creamy consistency a bit here by pairing them with grapefruit. It's an unexpected yet completely delicious combination. Paired with farro and hearts of palm, this bright salad is surprisingly hearty and totally clean. **Serves 4**

1 cup uncooked farro, rinsed and drained
3 cups water
3 cups mixed baby greens
One 14-ounce can hearts of palm, drained and thinly sliced on the diagonal
1 pink grapefruit, peeled and segmented
½ ripe avocado, thinly sliced

HONEY "SOY" VINAIGRETTE
3 tablespoons fresh lemon juice
2 tablespoons Bragg Liquid Aminos
2 tablespoons extra-virgin olive oil
2 teaspoons raw or manuka honey

In a medium saucepan over medium-high heat, combine the farro and water and bring to a boil. Reduce to a simmer, and cook for about 10 minutes, or until the farro is tender. Drain excess liquid, and set aside.

In a large bowl, whisk together the lemon juice, Bragg Liquid Aminos, olive oil, and honey. Add the cooked farro, mixed baby greens, and hearts of palm to the bowl and toss well to coat with the vinaigrette. Gently fold in the grapefruit segments and top with the avocado slices. Serve immediately.

CLEAN GREEN TIP: Eat more grapefruit! Grapefruit has been shown to help boost weight loss and is packed with vitamins A, C, and B_6.

AVOCADO-KALE
CAESAR SALAD

This perfect to-die-for pairing of supergreen superfoods is also supersimple to throw together—kale, apple, and avocado, with some hemp seeds for added omegas. Top with some tangy Light Caesar Dressing and—voilà!—a weeknight dinner in a hot sec! **Serves 4**

1 bunch lacinato kale, tough ribs removed, leaves torn

½ Fuji apple, halved and thinly sliced into half-moons

1 avocado, cut into 1-inch cubes

2 tablespoons hulled hemp seeds

LIGHT CAESAR DRESSING

2 tablespoons olive oil mayonnaise

1 tablespoon Dijon mustard

2 tablespoons fresh lemon juice

¼ teaspoon freshly ground black pepper

¼ teaspoon sea salt

1 tablespoon Worcestershire sauce (optional)

Prep the vegetables for the salad.

In a large bowl, whisk together the mayonnaise, mustard, lemon juice, pepper, sea salt, and Worcestershire sauce. Add the chopped kale and Fuji apple slices to the bowl and toss well to coat with the vinaigrette. Plate the salad and top with the avocado cubes and hulled hemp seeds.

SHAVED BRUSSELS SPROUTS SALAD

Delicious Brussels sprouts are finally getting their 15 minutes these days—I see them on restaurant menus everywhere! Brussels have an earthy flavor and a hefty texture—while being loaded with vitamin K, C, and folate. While we tend to sauté or roast Brussels sprouts most of the time, I love to prepare this raw, shaved Brussels sprouts salad, which really brings out the vegetable's unique texture and nutty flavor. I think you're going to love it, too! **Serves 4 to 6**

1½ pounds Brussels sprouts, thinly sliced
½ cup cored, halved, and thinly sliced Bartlett pear
½ cup raw walnut pieces
2 tablespoons crumbled blue cheese (optional)

HONEY-MUSTARD DRESSING
2 teaspoons raw or manuka honey
1 tablespoon Dijon mustard
3 tablespoons balsamic vinegar
3 tablespoons extra-virgin olive oil
½ teaspoon sea salt

Wash the Brussels sprouts and pat dry. Thinly slice the sprouts on a mandoline to a thickness of ⅛ inch. If you do not have a mandoline, use a sharp knife.

In a large bowl, whisk together the honey, mustard, vinegar, olive oil, and salt. Add the sliced Brussels sprouts and toss to coat with the dressing. Add the pear slices, walnuts, and blue cheese, if using. Serve immediately.

CURLY KALE WITH
TAHINI GARLIC DRESSING

On an overnight trip to shoot the morning news in Seattle, my man called and asked what I was eating that night for dinner. My response was, "Kale on kale." I had purchased three different kale salads to sample. The one that inspired this recipe was a superbasic kale and tahini salad that was outstanding. The memory of those bites led me to re-create my own version in my New York City kitchen, spreading kale love from coast to coast. **Serves 4**

5 cups curly kale, stems removed, leaves roughly chopped into bite-size pieces

TAHINI GARLIC DRESSING

¼ cup plus 1 tablespoon tahini paste*

2 teaspoons Bragg Liquid Aminos or reduced-sodium tamari soy sauce

1 garlic clove, finely minced

3 tablespoons fresh lemon juice

2 tablespoons raw apple cider vinegar

1 tablespoon nutritional yeast

Put all the ingredients for the dressing into a blender or food processor and blend until smooth. Pour the dressing into a large bowl and add the chopped kale. Toss to coat with your hands, massaging the dressing into the kale.

CLEAN GREEN TIP: Go ahead and massage that sexy kale. When you massage the leaves they soften up a bit and absorb more of the dressing, creating a more delicious salad. And, unlike with soft lettuces, you can also dress this salad a few hours before serving, cover, and hold in the fridge until dinner. Do you love extra-creamy kale salads? Opt for 1 additional tablespoon of tahini paste and mix well to combine.

---

* There's is a *big* difference between "tahini sauce" and "tahini/tahini paste." Tahini sauce = tahini paste plus ingredients like oil, lemon, garlic, salt. Tahini paste = straight-up, 100 percent pure ground sesame seeds.

CANDICE'S DANDELION GREENS
AND CURRY QUINOA SALAD

This salad and I have a love affair. With the sweet grilled corn, bitter dandelion greens, fresh mint, chewy quinoa, and the salty-sweet mix from the tamari and honey in the dressing, you'll fall in love with this full-meal salad, as well. **Serves 4**

1 cup uncooked quinoa

2 cups water

1 cup dandelion greens, roughly chopped,
    or wild baby arugula is just fine!

1 shallot, thinly sliced on a mandoline

1 cup grilled sweet corn kernels (about 1½ ears of corn, shaved)

2 tablespoons fresh mint leaves, stems removed

6 to 7 ounces firm marinated organic tofu or
    savory baked organic tofu, cubed

TAMARI HONEY DRESSING

2 tablespoons extra-virgin olive oil

1 tablespoon reduced-sodium tamari soy sauce, or more as needed

1 teaspoon curry powder (use more if desired!)

Juice of 1 lime

1 tablespoon grade A honey

In a medium saucepan, cook the quinoa with the water until all of the water has been absorbed and the quinoa is fully cooked and fluffy, about 15 minutes. Set aside to cool.

In a large bowl, whisk together the olive oil, tamari soy sauce, curry powder, lime juice, and honey. Add the quinoa, dandelion greens, shallots, shaved corn, mint, and cubed tofu to the bowl and toss well to coat with the dressing.

SUPERFOOD COCONUT CURRY SALMON SALAD

This recipe is for all of the busy women out there—supermoms, superworkers, superwomen deserve superfoods. Cook the salmon and the quinoa a day ahead, and throw this salad together in minutes on a weeknight. You could make it vegetarian if you prefer by swapping out the salmon for tofu—the marinade will still work perfectly! **Serves 4**

Coconut oil or olive oil cooking spray, for the baking dish

SALMON MARINADE

1 pound wild salmon fillet
1 tablespoon extra-virgin olive oil
½ teaspoon curry powder (add more if desired!)
1 tablespoon fresh lemon juice
1 teaspoon dried oregano, or 2 tablespoons fresh oregano
2 teaspoons reduced-sodium tamari soy sauce

COCONUT CURRY DRESSING

1 tablespoon unrefined coconut oil, at room temperature
1 teaspoon curry powder
3 tablespoons fresh lemon juice
1 teaspoon raw or manuka honey
2 tablespoons reduced-sodium tamari soy sauce

SALAD

2 cups lacinato kale leaves, finely chopped
2 cups cooked quinoa
¼ red onion, thinly sliced

Preheat the oven to 350°F. Coat a 9 x 13-inch baking dish with coconut oil or olive oil cooking spray and set aside.

In a medium bowl, whisk together the olive oil, curry, lemon juice, oregano, and tamari soy sauce. Place the salmon into a nonreactive container or baking dish with a lid, and pour the marinade over the top. Using a cooking brush, baste the salmon with the marinade, cover, and place into the fridge for about 30 minutes.

Remove the salmon from the fridge, and transfer to the prepared baking dish. Bake, on middle rack, for about 15 minutes. Remove from the oven and let cool slightly. The salmon should feel slightly firm to the touch.

Meanwhile, in a large bowl, whisk together the coconut oil, curry powder, lemon juice, honey, and tamari soy sauce until well combined. Add the kale, quinoa, and red onion to the bowl and toss gently to coat with the dressing. Flake in the cooked and slightly cooled salmon with fork, and toss to combine.

CLEAN GREEN TIP: Delicious unrefined coconut oil will solidify when below 76°F and will melt when above 76°F. For dressings, you always want to melt the coconut oil to a liquid consistency.

TOFU CURRY AND GREENS SALAD

This salad is packed with two clean-eating favorites: greens and protein. If you're not a huge curry fan, never fear, you can swap in my Lemon Olive Oil Dressing (see page 100) or my divine Clean Green Goddess Dressing (page 273)— both perfectly delicious options with this salad. **Serves 4**

6 to 7 ounces baked savory organic tofu (firm or extra-firm), cubed
3 celery stalks with leaves, leaves reserved, stalks finely diced
¼ red onion, finely diced
2¾ cups lacinato kale leaves, finely shredded, or mizuna leaves, torn
¼ cup dried cranberries
¼ cup raw walnuts, crushed
⅛ teaspoon sea salt (optional)

CURRY-DIJON DRESSING
2 tablespoons Dijon mustard
2 tablespoons olive oil mayonnaise
1 tablespoon fresh lemon juice
1 tablespoon curry powder

First, make the dressing: In a large bowl, whisk together the mustard, mayonnaise, lemon juice, and curry powder until well combined. Add the cubed tofu and toss to coat.

Add the diced celery, red onion, and kale to the curry tofu mixture. Fold in the dried cranberries, walnuts, and sea salt (if using). Top with the reserved celery leaves and serve.

CLEAN GREEN TIP: Celery greens are packed with flavor and nutrients. They can take the place of parsley in any dish. Toss them into salads, as well as smoothies!

MACROBIOTIC
HIJIKI-AVOCADO SALAD

Macrobiotic foods are naturally clean and detoxifying—they are plant-based and include sea vegetables, local produce, healthy grains, and fermented foods. Seaweed, naturally full of iodine, vitamin C, manganese, and vitamin B_2, is clean eating's best friend! I like to prepare macrobiotic meals after a period of food indulgence, such as the holidays or a vacation, as a way of resetting and balancing my body. Try this salad in your week of clean eating and you'll love the way you feel! **Serves 3**

1 cup soaked/reconstituted hijiki seaweed,* drained
   (measure: ¼ cup + 1 tablespoon dried hijki with ¾ cup water)
2 cups cooked quinoa
One 15-ounce can adzuki beans, rinsed and drained
1 ripe avocado, pitted and cut into cubes

DRESSING
2 tablespoons Bragg Liquid Aminos or reduced-sodium tamari soy sauce
¼ cup rice vinegar
1 tablespoon toasted sesame oil

In a medium bowl, soak and reconstitute ¼ cup, plus one tablespoon dried hijiki in ¾ cup water for about 15–20 minutes. Drain all excess liquid.

In a large bowl, whisk together the Bragg Liquid Aminos or reduced-sodium tamari soy sauce, rice vinegar, and toasted sesame oil. Add the reconstituted hijiki, quinoa, and adzuki beans to the dressing, and toss to coat. Top with avocado cubes and serve immediately.

CLEAN GREEN TIP: Adzuki beans (also referred to as azuki beans) are a delicious Japanese red bean that is packed with protein, potassium, and fiber. I love tossing these beans with rice, adding them to grain salads, and making them into sweet pastes for Japanese-style desserts. Mmmm, I love them!

* You can sub hijiki seaweed for 1 cup of reconstituted arame seaweed, as well!

6

CLEAN GREEN
SOUPS

THE MOST IMPORTANT THING YOU CAN TEACH
ANYONE IS TO THINK FOR YOURSELF WHEN MAKING
A DECISION ABOUT DIET AND LIFESTYLE.

—Michio Kushi

KALE CHICKEN NOODLE SOUP

Make chicken noodle soup like your grandmother did: with leftovers! Throw in your leftover chicken, a few handfuls of kale (and any other veggies that happen to be in your fridge), and use pantry staples to make this classic American comfort food. There's nothing like curling up with a warm bowl of chicken noodle soup on a cold day! **Serves 6**

2 tablespoons extra-virgin olive oil
1 small yellow onion, finely diced
2 carrots, peeled, halved, and thinly sliced into half-moons
1 leek, white and light green parts only, halved lengthwise, rinsed, and thinly sliced into half-moons
2 garlic cloves, thinly sliced
2 sprigs fresh thyme
8 cups low-sodium chicken or vegetable broth (make your own at home!)
½ teaspoon sea salt
2 cups uncooked egg noodles or pasta shells, or try barley or quinoa, or gluten-free varieties
1 cup thinly sliced lacinato kale leaves
1 cup leftover shredded rotisserie chicken
Lime wedges or sriracha sauce, for serving (optional)

In a large stockpot, warm the olive oil over medium heat. Add the onion and cook for 8 minutes until fragrant and soft. Reduce the heat to low and add the carrots, leeks, garlic, and thyme. Continue cooking, stirring occasionally, until the vegetables are tender and golden brown, 25 to 30 minutes.

Pour the broth over the sautéed vegetables and bring to a simmer. Add the pasta and cook for 6 to 8 minutes more until the pasta is cooked through. Add the kale and the shredded chicken and cook until the kale has wilted and the chicken is warmed through. Remove the thyme sprigs.

Serve the soup hot and enjoy with a squeeze of lime or sriracha sauce.

PARSNIP AND LEEK
DETOX SOUP

Parsnips are delicious and earthy root vegetables packed with fiber, protein, and vitamin C. I love pairing this nutrient-rich veggie with leeks and grated fresh ginger for a superclean, super-anti-inflammatory, and delicious soup. To add an extra detox boost to this recipe, I finish the soup with apple cider vinegar. **Serves 6**

2 tablespoons extra-virgin olive oil
1 yellow onion, finely diced
4 garlic cloves, minced
2 leeks, white and light green parts only,
    halved and sliced into ¼-inch half-moons
4 parsnips, peeled and cut on the diagonal into ½-inch slices
1 tablespoon peeled and grated fresh ginger
1 teaspoon ground cumin
8 cups low-sodium chicken (or use vegetable broth to make vegan)
1 cup organic quinoa or rice pasta (optional)
1½ cups shredded kale leaves (tough stems removed)
¾ teaspoon sea salt
2 tablespoons raw, unfiltered apple cider vinegar

In a large pot, warm the olive oil over medium-low heat. Add the onion, garlic, and leeks and sauté until the onion is soft and leeks are lightly brown, 8 to 10 minutes. Add the parsnips, and sauté, stirring occasionally, until light golden in color, about 20 minutes.

Add the fresh ginger and the cumin and cook, stirring, until fragrant. Pour in the broth and bring to a boil. Reduce the heat to medium-low and let simmer, for about 30 minutes.

Add the quinoa or the rice pasta, if using, and cook for about 10 minutes, or until the pasta is cooked through. Toss in the shredded kale, and season to taste with sea salt. Cook just until kale is slightly wilted. Stir in the apple cider vinegar and serve.

CLEAN GREEN MINESTRONE

With tomatoes for lycopene and vitamin C, chickpeas for protein, and arugula for vitamins A, C, and K, this is one minestrone that is 100 percent clean and green. No fillers, no additives, no preservatives. Add your choice of regular or gluten-free pasta, and finish it all off with a drizzle of balsamic vinegar for a bowl of hearty, healthy deliciousness. **Serves 6 to 8**

2 tablespoons extra-virgin olive oil
1 large yellow onion, finely diced
2 garlic cloves, thinly sliced
2 celery stalks, chopped
2 parsnips, peeled and sliced on the diagonal into ½-inch rounds
2 large organic red tomatoes, chopped
7 cups low-sodium vegetable broth
1 cup whole-wheat penne or barley (or try quinoa or rice pasta for a gluten-free option)
One 15-ounce can chickpeas (garbanzo beans), rinsed and drained
2 teaspoons sea salt
1 to 2 tablespoons balsamic vinegar
2 cups wild baby arugula or watercress to top

In a large stockpot, warm the olive oil over medium heat. Add the onion, and cook until soft and fragrant, about 8 minutes. Reduce the heat to medium-low, add the garlic, celery, and parsnips, and gently sweat for about 15 minutes.

Add in the chopped tomatoes and vegetable broth and bring to a boil. Lower to a simmer and cook for 12 minutes.

Add the pasta and continue to simmer for 10 to 15 minutes, or until the pasta is al dente.

Add the drained and rinsed chickpeas and cook until heated through. Season with sea salt to taste. Ladle the soup into bowls, finish with balsamic vinegar to taste (yum!), and top with the greens.

CLEAN GREEN TIP: Forget about crackers or croutons with zero nutrition! I like to top *my* soup bowl with double the amount of arugula or watercress, or sometimes use mizuna greens. The fresh greens add a beautiful pop of color and even more nutrients to the soup!

SPLIT PEA SOUP

My mom always made hearty foods for my dad, inspired by his Polish heritage—things like cabbage dumplings, pierogis, and split pea soup! This twist on my mom's classic incorporates red potatoes and smoked paprika. **Serves 6**

2 tablespoons extra-virgin olive oil
1 yellow onion, finely diced
2 bay leaves
2 medium carrots, peeled and cut into small diced pieces
1 large leek, trimmed, halved lengthwise,
   and thinly sliced into half-moons
5 garlic cloves, minced
8 cups low-sodium vegetable broth
2 cups dried organic split green peas
1 pound red potatoes, cut into ¼-inch diced pieces
1 tablespoon Bragg Liquid Aminos
1 teaspoon smoked paprika

In a large stockpot, warm the olive oil over medium-low heat. Add the onion and cook until soft and fragrant, 8 to 10 minutes. Add the bay leaves, carrots, and leeks and cook for another 8 minutes.

Add the vegetable broth and split green peas to the pot and bring to a boil. Reduce to a simmer and cook until the peas are tender, about 1 hour and 30 minutes, adding the diced potatoes after the first 20 minutes of cooking.

Remove and discard the bay leaves. Stir in the Bragg Liquid Aminos and smoked paprika and serve. Soup will be extra-thick. Yum!

RED LENTIL SOUP

Lentils are packed with protein, fiber, iron, and even potassium. This is a perfect post-workout soup—just one bowl will give you the protein fix your body is craving! I like to use red lentils in this recipe, but feel free to use any variety you prefer. They are all delicious and nutritious! **Serves 6**

2 tablespoons extra-virgin olive oil
½ yellow onion, finely chopped
4 garlic cloves, finely minced
2 carrots, peeled, chopped
2 celery stalks, chopped
1 bay leaf
8 cups low-sodium vegetable broth
1 cup dry red lentils, rinsed
½ teaspoon sea salt
2 to 4 tablespoons raw, unfiltered apple cider vinegar
   (add more if you love the taste!)
1½ cups thinly sliced lacinato kale leaves

In a medium stockpot, warm the olive oil over medium-low heat. Add the diced onion and sauté just until soft and fragrant, 8 to 10 minutes.

Reduce the heat to low, add the garlic, carrots, celery, and bay leaf, and cook for about 30 minutes, stirring occasionally.

Add the broth to the pot and bring the soup to a light simmer. Stir in lentils and cook for another 20 minutes, or until lentils are soft.

Remove and discard the bay leaf. Stir in the salt and vinegar and cook until kale is just slightly wilted. Serve with a clean green juice and enjoy that clean, lean protein fix!

CLEAN GREEN BARLEY WALNUT SOUP

This is one of my favorite soups in the book. With hearty barley, walnuts, fresh vegetables, and avocado, it is perfectly balanced in both flavor and texture. Fresh avocado slices and Liquid Aminos are the perfect way to finish it off. **Serves 6 to 8**

¾ cup uncooked hulled barley
1¾ cups water
2 tablespoons extra-virgin olive oil
1 yellow onion, finely chopped
2 carrots, peeled and chopped
2 celery stalks, chopped
2 bay leaves
8 cups low-sodium vegetable broth
¼ cup raw walnut pieces
¼ teaspoon freshly grated nutmeg
2 cups shredded lacinato kale leaves
1 ripe avocado, sliced
1 to 2 tablespoons Bragg Liquid Aminos

In a medium stockpot, combine the barley with the water and bring to a boil. Reduce to a simmer and cook until the grains are tender and the water has been absorbed. Cover and set aside.

In a large stockpot, warm the olive oil over medium-low heat. Add the onion and cook until softened, 8 to 10 minutes. Add the carrots, celery, and bay leaves and sauté until the veggies are soft, 10 to 12 minutes. Pour in the broth, bring the soup to a light simmer, and cook.

Stir in the reserved cooked barley, walnut pieces, and nutmeg and simmer for an additional 5 minutes.

Remove and discard the bay leaves. Stir in the kale and Bragg Liquid Aminos. Ladle the soup into bowls and top off with avocado slices. Feel free to add unfiltered, raw apple cider vinegar to finish, for some extra cleansing.

CLEAN GREEN TIP: If your vegetables stick to the bottom of the pot, add 2 tablespoons of broth at a time and scrape the browned bits up from the bottom—they will add extra flavor to the broth.

CREAMY COCONUT AND FRESH PEA MINT SOUP

This protein- and antioxidant-packed bright green soup is the perfect definition of clean and green. It is best served chilled or at room temperature, making it a refreshing, light meal for the warmer months. A dollop of Greek yogurt on top adds an indulgent, creamy texture and the added benefits of probiotics.

Serves 4; yields 5 cups

2 tablespoons extra-virgin olive oil
1 yellow onion, finely chopped
One 16-ounce package frozen peas, thawed
1 cup packed fresh mint leaves, plus more for optional garnish
¼ teaspoon sea salt
½ cup canned light coconut milk, plus 1 to 2 tablespoons for finishing
1½ cups low-sodium vegetable broth

OPTIONAL TOPPING
Greek yogurt (omit for dairy-free or vegan)

In a small sauté pan, warm the olive oil over medium heat. Add the onion and cook until fragrant, 10 to 12 minutes. Remove from the heat and set aside to cool slightly.

Add the cooled onion mixture to a blender or food processor, followed by the peas, mint leaves, and salt; blend to combine. Stream in the coconut milk and vegetable broth until the mixture has a nice, velvety soup consistency.

Serve the soup at room temperature or chilled with the extra coconut milk and mint to finish. Top with a dollop of Greek yogurt, if desired, for an extra boost of protein!

ROASTED KABOCHA SQUASH AND QUINOA SOUP

One of the great things about kabocha squash is that you don't need to peel it—you can eat the skin, which is full of nutrients. My mom used to make it for us when we were kids in Cali, but it wasn't until I moved to the East Coast that I really began to fall in love with this warm, winter squash. There is nothing better than a bowl of this soup on a rainy, chilly afternoon. **Serves 4**

2 tablespoons extra-virgin olive oil
1 yellow onion, finely diced
2 bay leaves
2 crushed garlic cloves
1 large kabocha squash, unpeeled, halved, and cut into ¾-inch cubes
8 cups low-sodium vegetable broth
¾ cup uncooked quinoa
1 tablespoons Bragg Liquid Aminos
½ cup shredded lacinato kale leaves

In a large stockpot, warm the extra-virgin olive oil over medium-low heat. Add the onion and cook until soft, 8 to 10 minutes. Add the crushed garlic and bay leaves and sauté for an additional 5 minutes until fragrant.

Add the kabocha and cook for about 8 minutes, or until the squash begins to develop some color.

Pour in the broth and bring the soup to a boil. Turn heat to low and reduce to a simmer. Simmer for about 15 minutes. Adjust the heat to medium-low, add the quinoa, and simmer for an additional 15 minutes.

Stir in the Bragg Liquid Aminos, add the shredded kale, and heat just until the kale has wilted slightly. Serve immediately, paired with some matcha green tea for extra cleansing!

7

CLEAN GREEN SNACKS

THE INVENTOR OF SODA CRACKERS
HAS A PLACE IN HELL.
—*Martin H. Fischer*

ROASTED KALE CHIPS

These delicious kale chips are low in calories and packed full of vitamins and minerals. When you want a crunchy snack, ditch the expensive packaged kale chips and make these crispy treats in your own oven. You can season them however you'd like—the garlic and cayenne combo below is one of my favorites, but get creative, I'm also partial to seasoning with Japanese spices like togarashi or furikake. **Serves 6; yields 5 cups**

8 packed cups curly kale, stems removed, leaves torn into uniform chip-size pieces
2 tablespoons reduced-sodium tamari soy sauce
2 tablespoons toasted sesame oil
2 teaspoons granulated garlic powder
½ teaspoon chili powder or cayenne pepper

Preheat the oven to 300°F. Line 2 to 3 baking sheets with parchment paper or aluminum foil. Place the torn kale onto the lined sheets, making sure the pieces don't overlap too much. Drizzle with the tamari soy sauce and sesame oil, and sprinkle with the garlic powder and chili powder or cayenne, adding more if you prefer some heat. Toss to coat.

Bake the kale chips for 20 minutes, or until crisp, rotating the baking sheets halfway through the baking time. Remove from the oven and allow to cool and crisp.

CLEAN GREEN TIP: Be sure to tear the kale pieces into uniform sizes and spread them in an even single layer on each baking sheet for best results. The chips won't get as crispy if you overcrowd them on the baking sheet.

WASABI-SPICED CASHEWS

With a simple dash of wasabi and ginger, plain old raw cashews get an exotic hit of flavor along with some anti-inflammatory benefits. Eating clean never tasted so unexpectedly delicious! **Serves 8**

3 cups whole, raw cashews
1 egg white
1 tablespoon unrefined coconut oil
6 tablespoons high-quality powdered wasabi
1 teaspoon ginger powder
1½ teaspoons sea salt

Preheat the oven to 375°F. Place the nuts on an ungreased baking sheet and pre-roast for 8 to 10 minutes until slightly golden. Remove from oven and let cool. Reduce the oven temperature to 350°F. Line a baking sheet with parchment paper.

In a large bowl, whisk together the egg white, unrefined coconut oil, wasabi powder, ginger powder, and sea salt. Add the cooled cashews to the bowl and toss to coat.

Transfer the nuts to the lined baking sheet. Bake in the oven at 350°F for 10 to 12 minutes.

Remove the nuts from the oven and allow to cool. The nuts can be stored in an airtight container for up to 2 weeks.

CLEAN GREEN TIP: When removing these cashews from the oven, proceed with caution! When the smell of the hot wasabi hits you in the eyes and nose, it can overwhelm, to say the least. I recommend opening the oven door slowly and turning your head to the side!

SPICY EDAMAME
HUMMUS

This to-die-for creamy and rich clean green dip is perfect for party app pleasing. The thick texture from the edamame and chickpeas combined with the spiciness from the sriracha make it a perfect balance for fresh crudités like cucumber slices, radishes, jicama, and even apple slices. **Serves 6 to 8; yields 3 cups**

2½ cups frozen, organic shelled edamame, thawed
2 cups chickpeas (garbanzo beans), rinsed and drained
2 roasted garlic cloves
2 tablespoons fresh lemon juice
1 tablespoon extra-virgin olive oil
1 tablespoon reduced-sodium tamari soy sauce
2 tablespoons sriracha sauce

Place the edamame, chickpeas, roasted garlic, lemon juice, extra-virgin olive oil, tamari soy sauce, and sriracha sauce in a food processor or blender and pulse until smooth.

Serve alongside your favorite crudité platter, or enjoy slathered on toasted bread and sandwiches. This hummus can be stored in the fridge, in an airtight container, for up to a week.

CLEAN GREEN GUACAMOLE AND HOMEMADE CHILI-LIME CHIPS

Delicious, ripe, creamy, green, heart-healthy avocados—nature's perfect food—just got a little more delicious with the pairing of home-baked tortilla chips. With the sneaky addition of arugula in this dip, it is a fabulously delicious way to indulge in chips and guac without the guilt. **Serves 8; yields 2 cups**

CHIPS

Coconut oil or olive oil cooking spray, for the baking sheets
2 teaspoons chili powder
½ teaspoon sea salt
4 teaspoons extra-virgin olive oil
2 tablespoons lime juice
Eight 8-inch whole-wheat or corn flour tortillas

GUACAMOLE

3 avocados, halved and pitted, peeled and cubed
¼ small red onion, finely diced
1½ tablespoons reduced-sodium tamari soy sauce
Juice of ½ lime
1 cup wild baby arugula
2 tablespoons fresh cilantro, finely chopped or whole leaves (optional)

Preheat the oven to 350°F. Line two rimmed baking sheets with parchment paper or aluminum foil, and coat with coconut oil or olive oil cooking spray.

In a small bowl, whisk together the chili powder, salt, olive oil, and lime juice. Set aside.

Place a tortilla on a cutting board and cut it into quarters, and then into eighths, making 8 triangles from each tortilla. Repeat with the remaining tortillas and place them on the baking sheets so the triangles are just barely touching one another. (You may need to toast them in 2 batches.) Brush the tortillas with the spice mixture.

Bake the tortillas until browned and crisp, 12 to 14 minutes, rotating the baking sheet midway through the baking. Remove them from the oven and set aside to cool completely before transferring to a large serving bowl. Sprinkle with additional sea salt, if needed.

While the chips are cooling, make the guacamole: Place the avocados in a medium bowl. Using a fork, gently smash and stir the avocado, breaking it up into a chunky mass, leaving some avocado bits whole. Add the onion, tamari soy sauce, and lime juice and stir to combine. Top with wild arugula and the cilantro, if using. Taste with a chip, and add more salt if needed. Serve up the party immediately!

TAHINI AVOCADO
CHICKPEA DIP

This is such a simple and delicious dip to throw together anytime company is coming over. I always keep canned chickpeas on hand just so I can make a quick hummus or dip in a pinch. If you like making hummus and guacamole, this dip is your new bestie for sure. **Serves 6**

1 avocado, halved, pitted, peeled, and cubed
1 can chickpeas (garbanzo beans), rinsed and drained
3 tablespoons tahini paste (see footnote page 108)
2 teaspoons Bragg Liquid Aminos

In a medium bowl, mash the chickpeas with a fork or potato masher. Add the avocado and continue mashing until the chickpeas and avocado are combined. Stir in the tahini paste and Bragg Liquid Aminos and mix to incorporate.

Serve the dip alongside your choice of crudités, toasted bread, or rice crackers. Add a squeeze of fresh lemon to brighten it up after refrigerating (and to add a hit of vitamin C!).

SWEET POTATO FRIES WITH HOMEMADE CURRY KETCHUP

These delicious classic sweet potato fries are filled with vitamin A, beta-carotene, and filling fiber. YUM. Of course you can serve these with plain old ketchup, but the extra effort of making my curry ketchup from scratch is really worth it—the pairing of curry and sweet potatoes is totally heaven!

Serves 4 to 6

2 pounds sweet potatoes
2 tablespoons unrefined coconut oil
1 tablespoon granulated garlic powder
½ teaspoon ginger powder
½ teaspoon sea salt
Homemade Curry Ketchup (page 266)

Preheat the oven to 375°F. Line two baking sheets with aluminum foil.

Cut the sweet potatoes into ½-inch-thick wedges. Transfer to a large bowl.

In a small saucepan, melt the coconut oil over low heat. Pour the coconut oil onto the potatoes and sprinkle on the garlic powder, ginger, and salt and toss to coat.

Spread out the coated potatoes evenly on the lined baking sheets. Roast for about 40 minutes, or until the potatoes are golden brown and crispy. Serve along with the curry ketchup, and dip 'em while they're hot!

CLEAN GREEN
HERBED CASHEWS

These delicious cashews are made with dried dill, spirulina powder, tamari soy sauce, and decadent coconut oil. Remember, all nuts are packed with nutrition when raw, but when you need a pick-me-up kinda recipe, just make a big batch of these delicious roasted green cashews to much on! **Serves 6**

1 pound raw cashews (about 3 cups)
1 tablespoon coconut oil, plus 1 teaspoon, melted (mmmm, yum!)
2 tablespoons reduced-sodium tamari soy sauce
1 tablespoon dried oregano
2 tablespoons granulated garlic powder
1 tablespoon dried dill
½ teaspoon spirulina powder (optional)

Preheat the oven to 375°F. Place the nuts on an ungreased baking sheet and pre-roast for 8 to 10 minutes until slightly golden. Remove from the oven and let cool. Reduce the oven temperature to 350°F. Line baking sheets with parchment paper.

To a medium bowl, add the melted unrefined coconut oil, tamari soy sauce, 2 teaspoons of the dried oregano, 1 tablespoon of the garlic powder, and 2 teaspoons of the dried dill and mix well to combine. Add the cooled nuts to the bowl and toss well to coat.

Transfer the nuts to the lined baking sheets and bake in the oven at 350°F for 10 minutes.

Remove the nuts from the oven and sprinkle with the remaining 1 teaspoon oregano, 1 tablespoon garlic powder, 1 teaspoon dried dill, and the spirulina powder, if using. Return the nuts to the oven for 2 additional minutes.

These nuts are delicious served warm, but can also be stored in an airtight container for up to 2 weeks.

8

CLEAN GREEN
BURGERS AND
SANDWICHES

TOO FEW PEOPLE UNDERSTAND
A REALLY GOOD SANDWICH.

—James Beard

SWEET POTATO AVOCADO BURGER

This California-style burger was tested numerous times to perfect and ensure that the patties are crisp, firm, tasty, and delicious. The combination of rolled oats, raw walnuts, chia seeds, and flaxseed meal will keep you totally full on protein and fiber. Top with delicious avocado slices, and you've got a veggie burger unlike any you've ever tasted! The patties will last for up to a week, refrigerated.

Serves 8 to 10; yields 13 to 15 small patties

WET INGREDIENTS

2 pounds sweet potato cubes, roasted (see step one)

2 tablespoons extra-virgin olive oil

1 tablespoon granulated garlic powder

2 tablespoons reduced-sodium tamari soy sauce

3 tablespoons Worcestershire sauce (omit for vegan)

¼ yellow onion, roughly chopped

1 cup chickpeas (garbanzo beans),
    rinsed and drained

DRY INGREDIENTS

1¼ cups organic rolled oats

¾ cup raw walnuts, crushed

¾ cup flaxseed meal

FOR COOKING

2 tablespoons unrefined coconut oil

FOR SERVING

Whole-wheat or gluten-free buns

2 ripe avocados, thinly sliced (2 to 3 slices per burger)

1 teaspoon Worcestershire sauce (per burger; omit for vegan)

¼ red onion, thinly sliced

1 to 2 torn lacinato kale leaves per burger

Dijon mustard

Olive oil mayonnaise (omit for vegan)

Wash and pat your sweet potatoes dry. Cut the sweet potatoes into small 1-inch cubes. Roast the sweet potato cubes with 2 tablespoons extra-virgin olive oil, 1 tablespoon granulated garlic powder, and ½ teaspoon salt. Place onto a sheet tray and roast at 375°F for approximately 40 minutes, remove from the oven, and cool slightly.

In a food processor, add the roasted/cooked sweet potato, tamari soy sauce, and Worcestershire sauce; pulse to combine. Add the onion and chickpeas and pulse until fully combined, periodically stopping the food processor and using a spatula or wooden spoon to move the mixture around. Mix just until the chickpeas and onion are fully incorporated; look for the consistency of mashed potatoes. Do not overmix.

Meanwhile, in a large bowl, combine the oats, walnuts, chia seeds, and flaxseed meal.

Remove the sweet potato mixture from the food processor and fold into the dry ingredients. Measure out ⅓ cup of the mixture at a time and, using your hands, form into round burger-shaped patties.

In a medium sauté pan, heat the coconut oil over medium heat. Add the patties and sauté for about 4 minutes per side, or until they are warmed through and golden brown on each side.

To serve, place the patties on toasted buns, if desired, and add your choice of toppings, I love avocado, kale, and Worcestershire sauce.

AVOCADO CHICKPEA
KALE SANDWICH

This simple and clean sandwich can be served open-faced, just like toast, or slap it together to create a hearty and wholesome clean green sandwich. When a recipe is this simple, the quality of the ingredients really matters—look for the freshest pumpernickel bread and the ripest, juiciest tomatoes you can find! **Serves 2; half sandwich for each person**

Coconut oil or olive oil cooking spray, for the skillet
2 slices pumpernickel bread, toasted
¼ cup Tahini Avocado Chickpea Dip (page 140)
4 leaves lacinato or curly kale
4 thinly sliced tomato slices
⅛ red onion, thinly sliced
Maldon sea salt, to finish

First, toast the bread: Coat a medium skillet with a coconut oil or olive oil cooking spray and place over medium heat. Add the bread slices to the skillet and toast on both sides, 1 to 2 minutes per side. Remove the toast from the skillet and place on a clean work surface.

To assemble the sandwich, spread 1 tablespoon of the dip onto each slice of bread. Top with kale, sliced tomato, red onion, and a touch of sea salt to finish. Add the second toast slice on the top, and slice the sandwich diagonally in half. Serve to share!

VEGAN CHICKPEA CURRY BURGER

This recipe will have everyone, including your super-carnivore friends (yes, that means the guys!) wanting more. Chickpeas and rolled oats are packed with protein and fiber and the curry and tamari lend the patty an earthy, savory flavor. Pair it with crisp, fresh tomato slices and Bibb lettuce, and this clean green is as satisfying as any traditional burger. Enjoy it with Sweet Potato Fries (page 141) for a complete meal. **Serves 6; yields about 6 to 7 medium patties**

Coconut oil or olive oil cooking spray,
    for the baking sheet
One 15-ounce can chickpeas (garbanzo beans),
    rinsed and drained
½ red onion, finely diced
1 cup organic rolled oats
½ cup shelled, raw walnuts
2 teaspoons curry powder
½ teaspoon freshly grated nutmeg
2 tablespoons flaxseed meal
3 tablespoons reduced-sodium tamari soy sauce
½ cup chopped fresh parsley

FOR SERVING

5 soft whole-wheat burger buns, potato rolls,
    or gluten-free buns, split
Olive oil mayonnaise, as needed
Dijon mustard, as needed
1 ripe tomato, thinly sliced
1 ripe avocado, thinly sliced
7 crisp Boston or Bibb lettuce leaves

Preheat the oven to 350°F degrees. Line a large baking sheet with parchment paper, and generously coat with coconut oil spray.

In a food processor, add the chickpeas, red onion, rolled oats, walnuts, curry powder, nutmeg, flaxseed meal, tamari soy sauce, and parsley; pulse for 45 seconds to 1 minute, or until completely combined. Look for the consistency of mashed potatoes.

Measure out ⅓ cup of the mixture at a time and, using clean hands, form into round burger-shaped patties. Once you have formed all of the patties, place them onto the prepared baking sheet. To make both sides golden, spray the top of each patty with coconut or olive oil spray and bake for 20 minutes on the middle rack. After 10 minutes, carefully flip the burgers, additionally spray the top of each patty with coconut or olive oil spray, and bake for the remaining 10 minutes. Remove the patties from the oven and let cool slightly. Watch your patties, as each oven varies.

To serve, place on toasted buns and add your choice of prepared toppings.

CLEAN GREEN TIP: When making this delicious chickpea burger, be sure to pulse just until a fine meal appears; if you blend too much, you'll make hummus!

CHIPOTLE
SALMON BURGER

This delicious omega-3, brain-boosting salmon burger is the tastiest way to have it all. Made from simple canned salmon (nothing fancy!), this is a budget-friendly way to enjoy all of the nutritional benefits salmon has to offer. The Creamy Chive Sauce is like a more-delicious version of tartar sauce—and pairs perfectly with any type of fish. **Serves 4; yields about 12 mini-burger patties**

2 tablespoons olive oil mayonnaise

2 tablespoons fresh lime juice

3 tablespoons reduced-sodium tamari soy sauce

½ red bell pepper, seeded, ribs removed, and finely chopped

½ small red onion, finely chopped

2 tablespoons chipotle peppers in adobo sauce, finely chopped (omit for kids)

½ cup panko bread crumbs

½ cup flaxseed meal

1 large egg, beaten

Three 5- to 6-ounce cans high-quality boneless and skinless wild salmon, drained

2 tablespoons extra-virgin olive oil

FOR SERVING

1 package regular or gluten-free mini-slider buns, toasted

12 small kale leaves, tough ribs or stems removed, torn

½ red onion, thinly sliced

CREAMY CHIVE SAUCE

½ cup Greek yogurt

¼ cup fresh chives, finely sliced on the diagonal

1 tablespoon Worcestershire sauce

In a medium bowl, whisk together the mayonnaise, lime juice, and soy sauce. Add the bell pepper, onion, and chopped chipotle peppers, and stir until well combined. Fold in the panko, flaxseed, and beaten egg. Gently fold in the salmon.

Divide the mixture into six equal parts and, using clean hands, shape each into a ball. Pat each ball into 2½-inch-wide and ¾-inch-thick burger patties. Place the patties into an airtight container and cover.

Heat a medium grill pan or cast-iron skillet over medium-high heat. Add the olive oil, reduce the heat to medium, and cook the patties, in batches, until golden brown, 2 to 3 minutes. Gently turn them over and brown the opposite sides for an additional 2 to 3 minutes. Transfer the cooked patties to a paper towel–lined plate while you prepare the sauce.

In a small bowl, whisk together the yogurt, chives, and Worcestershire sauce.

To serve, place each burger on a toasted bun, smear on a dollop of the sauce, and layer on the kale and thinly sliced red onion.

CLEAN GREEN TIP: Instead of making burgers, you can shape the salmon mixture into mini–salmon cakes for bite-size party appetizers. Top with a little dollop of creamy chive sauce and watch your guests devour these bites!

BISON BURGER WITH HOMEMADE APPLE CIDER QUICK PICKLES

Protein-packed, grass-fed bison is even leaner than 90 percent lean beef, making it a great healthy burger option. Bison also packs more flavor than beef, and with the addition of sautéed onions and Worcestershire for a juicy flavor boost, this cleaner, leaner burger combo is sure to satisfy any serious burger craving.

Serves 5 (about 5 burger patties)

2 tablespoons unrefined coconut oil, plus 2 teaspoons to cook the burgers

1 yellow onion, finely diced

1 pound lean ground bison

2 tablespoons reduced-sodium tamari soy sauce

1 tablespoon Worcestershire sauce

1 teaspoon granulated garlic powder

¼ teaspoon freshly ground black pepper

FOR SERVING

5 soft whole-wheat or gluten-free burger buns or potato rolls, split

Olive oil mayonnaise, as needed

Dijon mustard, as needed

5 lacinato or curly kale leaves, stems removed, leaves torn

1 ripe tomato, thinly sliced

1 ripe avocado, thinly sliced

Homemade Apple Cider Quick Pickles (page 269)

In a large skillet over low heat, melt the 2 tablespoons of coconut oil. Add the onion, stirring occasionally, until light golden brown and caramelized, about 25 minutes. Remove from the heat and transfer the onions to a plate to cool slightly. Reserve the pan for cooking the burgers.

With clean hands, add the ground bison to a large bowl and season with the tamari soy sauce, Worcestershire sauce, garlic powder, and pepper. Add the cooled onions and gently fold them into the meat, using your clean hands. Shape the bison into five 1-inch-thick patties. Place the patties into an airtight container, using squares of foil or parchment paper to layer in between patties, and refrigerate for 30 minutes.

In the same skillet you used to cook the onions, heat the remaining 2 teaspoons coconut oil, add the patties, and cook over medium-high heat until deep brown outside and medium-rare inside, 4 to 5 minutes per side.

To serve, spread a touch of olive oil mayonnaise and Dijon mustard on each half of a bun. Toast the buns, mayonnaise and mustard side down, in the same skillet on medium-low heat. Transfer the burgers to the toasted buns, and top with the kale, tomato, avocado, and Homemade Apple Cider Vinegar Quick Pickles (page 269).

CURRY-APPLE-POTATO SALAD SANDWICH

Making sandwiches from leftovers shouldn't be reserved for your annual post-Thanksgiving turkey/cranberry monster sandwich—it is an everyday, cost-saving and time-saving strategy. Get creative with everything from roasted veggies to salmon, chicken, or even tofu. I love topping this sandwich with crisp, leafy, glowing greens like kale or watercress. **Serves 2**

About 1 cup leftover Roasted Curried Apple-Potato Salad (page 173)
2 slices rye bread, or your choice of bread!
Olive oil mayonnaise
1½ teaspoons unsalted butter
1 tablespoon Dijon mustard
2 tablespoons dried cranberries (1 tablespoon per sandwich)

TOPPING (OPTIONAL)
Chopped kale
Watercress

First, toast the bread: Lightly coat two slices of bread with mayonnaise on one side only. In a medium sauté pan over medium-low heat, melt the butter and toast the slices of rye bread for about 2 minutes on each side, or until crisp. Remove from the heat and place the toast on a clean work surface. Cut each slice of bread in half on the diagonal, creating four slices of toast. Spread a thin layer of Dijon on one half of each sandwich.

Top two slices of bread with a generous scoop of the potato salad. Top the salad with 1 tablespoon dried cranberries. Layer on the chopped kale or watercress, and place the other slice of toast on top to make a sandwich, slice in half, and indulge in every bite!

CLEAN GREEN AVOCADO GRILLED CHEESE

This recipe was originally a spinoff on my classic grilled cheese. I used to make hundreds of these at the Ritz-Carlton when I was cooking on the line. And, yes, we made them crustless and fancy-pants, calling them "Croque Monsieur Fingers," on the menu for $20 a pop! This improved version includes tomatoes, kale, and avocado—YUM. Pair with a bowl of soup and you will be in heaven. **Serves 4**

DIJONNAISE
2 tablespoons Dijon mustard
2 tablespoons olive oil mayonnaise

GRILLED CHEESE
1 tablespoon unsalted butter
8 slices whole-wheat, whole-grain, or gluten-free bread
8 ultrathin slices Gruyère or Asiago cheese
4 kale leaves, tough ribs or stems removed, leaves torn
1 ripe tomato, thinly sliced into 8 rounds, then cut into half-moons
1 ripe avocado, pitted, peeled, and thinly sliced
Maldon sea salt, to finish

In a small bowl, whisk together the mustard and mayonnaise to create the Dijonnaise. Spread on one side of each slice of bread.

Add the butter to a medium nonstick skillet and melt over medium heat. Add the bread slices (you should hear them sizzle when they hit the pan) and grill until browned, about 2 minutes. Flip over and brown the opposite sides, 1 to 1½ minutes longer (the second side usually browns more quickly than the first). Top each slice with cheese, and heat until the cheese starts to melt. Add the kale leaves, tomato, and avocado slices and top with a slice of bread. Once the cheese has fully melted, remove the pan from the heat.

Transfer the sandwiches to a cutting board and let them cool for 2 minutes before slicing. Cut into two diagonal pieces and serve immediately. Season with sea salt, if desired, pair with a glass of almond milk or a warm bowl of soup!

SMASHED AVOCADO AND SMOKED SALMON OVER PUMPERNICKEL

LS

This super-elegant yet simple recipe is a perfect five-minute bite you can prepare just before guests arrive for a brunch or lunch. Also packed with mood-boosting omegas from the salmon, consider this a "happy recipe." I know it is guaranteed to make you smile! **Serves 4**

4 slices pumpernickel bread, halved and toasted
1 tablespoon olive oil mayonnaise
Coconut oil or olive oil cooking spray, for the pan
1 ripe avocado, thinly sliced
¼ red onion, thinly sliced
4 ounces high-quality, wild smoked salmon
Greek yogurt, for dolloping
1½ teaspoons caraway (or fennel) seed

First, toast the bread: Lightly coat one side of each bread slice with the mayonnaise. Coat a medium sauté pan with coconut oil or olive oil cooking spray and place over medium-low heat. Add the bread slices to the pan and toast for about 2 minutes on each side, or until crisp. Repeat with all 4 slices of bread. Remove from heat and transfer the toast to a clean work surface. Cut each slice of bread in half on the diagonal, creating eight slices of toast, two for each person.

Arrange 2 to 3 thin slices of avocado on each piece of toast. Add the red onion slices next, then fold the smoked salmon on top. Add a dollop of Greek yogurt and a sprinkle of caraway seeds. Serve open-faced and fabulous.

CLEAN GREEN TIP: Smoked salmon and lox are actually two different types of fish. Both are fabulous, but: Lox is cured salmon (in a salt brine), traditionally sourced from the Pacific Ocean. Smoked Salmon is not cured and is prepared with Atlantic and Pacific salmon, both wild-caught and farm-raised. I recommend always purchasing wild-caught salmon for optimum flavor and health benefits.

9

CLEAN GREEN
SIDES

FILL YOUR PLATE WITH THE COLORS
OF THE RAINBOW. WHAT PLEASES THE EYE,
PLEASES THE BODY.

— Deepak Chopra

WARM POTATO AND WATERCRESS SALAD

Potato salad is the ultimate crowd pleaser, and perfect for any backyard barbecue, a sunny picnic, or an outdoor lunch with the fam. This healthier version of the original is made with olive oil mayonnaise, and incorporates one of our favorite supergreens, watercress, for a pop of color and a little crunch. **Serves 4**

1½ pounds unpeeled red potatoes
½ red onion, thinly sliced
1 bunch watercress leaves, washed and trimmed

DRESSING
2 tablespoons Dijon mustard
1 tablespoon olive oil mayonnaise
2 tablespoons fresh lemon juice
½ teaspoon freshly ground black pepper
½ teaspoon sea salt

In a large stockpot, boil the potatoes in water to cover until fork-tender, about 10 minutes. Drain and let cool.

While the potatoes are cooling, make the dressing: In a large bowl, whisk together the mustard, mayonnaise, lemon juice, pepper, and salt until well combined.

Cut the cooled potatoes into 1-inch cubes. Add the potatoes, onion, and watercress to the bowl with the dressing and toss gently to coat.

SUN-DRIED TOMATO AND TOFU FARRO SALAD

Farro has an earthy and unique flavor and is packed with protein and super-nutrients like fiber and iron. I like to use this ancient grain in salads and soups, as its hearty texture holds up well to whatever you mix it with. I use tofu in this salad to keep it vegan-green; other great options to try include salmon or even leftover rotisserie chicken. **Serves 4**

2 cups uncooked farro, rinsed

3 cups water

1 tablespoon extra-virgin olive oil

½ yellow onion, thinly sliced

2 blocks savory baked firm organic tofu (firm or extra-firm),
    cut into ¾-inch cubes

1 cup baby spinach, washed and dried

¼ cup sun-dried tomatoes, drained, rinsed, julienne sliced

¼ cup crumbled goat cheese (optional; omit if vegan or dairy-free)

BALSAMIC VINAIGRETTE

2 tablespoons extra-virgin olive oil

¼ cup balsamic vinegar

¾ teaspoon sea salt

Combine the farro and water in a medium saucepan and bring to a boil over high heat. Reduce the heat to low and simmer for about 15 minutes, or until all the liquid has been absorbed and the farro is cooked through. Cool slightly.

While the farro cooks, warm the oil in a medium sauté pan over medium-low heat and sauté the onion for 6 to 8 minutes until slightly golden. Add the cubed tofu and cook until warmed through, about 5 minutes. Remove from heat and set the mixture aside to cool slightly while you make the dressing.

In a large bowl, whisk together the oil, balsamic vinegar, and sea salt until well combined. Add the warm farro to the bowl and toss to combine with the dressing. Add the cooled onion-tofu mixture, baby spinach, and sun-dried tomatoes and toss again. Finish with the crumbled goat cheese, if using, and enjoy, gorgeous!

SAUTÉED SWISS CHARD WITH APPLES AND SUNFLOWER SEEDS

My mom used to sauté Swiss chard for us when we were kids, and I was always so drawn to its beautiful rainbow colors. I am still totally inspired by Mom's magic in the kitchen. This recipe is a perfect one to cook for kids and to get little hands involved in the kitchen, washing veggies, measuring out ingredients . . . and, of course, sampling! **Serves 4**

2 pounds Swiss chard, stem ends trimmed
1 tablespoon extra-virgin olive oil
1 small red onion, halved and thinly sliced
½ teaspoon sea salt
1 Fuji or Honeycrisp apple, cored and thinly sliced
1 tablespoon fresh lemon juice
¼ cup raw sunflower seeds

Place the washed Swiss chard on a cutting board. Using a sharp knife, cut the colorful stems from the leaves. Slice the stems crosswise into ¼-inch pieces and place them in a bowl. Stack the green leaves, roll them into a thick cigar shape, and slice them crosswise into ¼-inch-wide ribbons.

Heat the oil in a large nonstick skillet over medium-high heat. Add the onion and salt and cook, stirring often, until the onion begins to soften, 3 to 4 minutes. Stir in the chard stems and apple slices and cook until they start to soften, about 4 minutes. Add the greens and cook, stirring often, until they begin to wilt, about another 4 minutes. Finish with the lemon juice and turn the greens out onto a serving platter. Sprinkle the sunflower seeds over the top and serve hot.

SPICY BROCCOLI RABE
WITH GARLIC AND CHILI FLAKES

I love the distinctive, bitter taste of broccoli rabe, which also happens to be full of vitamins A, C, and folate. This delicate sister to the turnip cooks up in about seven minutes and is delicious paired with pasta like orecchiette, lean protein, or tofu and grains. Top with crushed red chili flakes for a little heat . . . yum!

Serves 4

3 tablespoons extra-virgin olive oil
½ yellow onion, finely chopped
3 garlic cloves, finely minced
1 bunch broccoli rabe (aka rapini), chopped into 1½-inch pieces on the diagonal
Two 6-ounce packages savory baked firm organic tofu (firm or extra-firm),
    cut into ¾-inch cubes
1 teaspoon crushed red chili flakes, more or less to your desired preference
1 cup cooked freekeh or farro (your choice of grains!)
1 teaspoon reduced-sodium tamari soy sauce
2 teaspoons fresh lemon juice

In a large sauté pan, warm 2 tablespoons of the extra-virgin olive oil over medium heat. Add the onion and garlic and cook over medium-low heat just until fragrant, about 5 minutes. Add the broccoli rabe, increase the heat to medium, and cook for about 2 minutes.

Add the tofu to the pan and cook for 2 more minutes. Add the chili flakes and the cooked freekeh or farro and toss to coat. Cook for another 3 minutes to warm all through.

Remove the pan from heat and stir in the remaining 1 tablespoon extra-virgin olive oil, soy sauce, and lemon juice. Serve hot alongside some grilled salmon or add more tofu to make it a full meal.

ROASTED BALSAMIC ROSEMARY POTATOES

This simple one-pan recipe is brightened up by the wonderful aromas and flavors of rosemary, garlic, and thyme. After the red potatoes are roasted with the herbs, the whole dish is finished off with a hit of creamy Greek yogurt and tangy balsamic vinegar. This side dish is my new fave of the bunch! Pair these potatoes with any protein, and a simple green salad like my Avocado-Kale Caesar Salad (page 105) for a clean and complete meal. **Serves 6**

3 pounds red potatoes, quartered

1 tablespoon plus 2 teaspoons extra-virgin olive oil

1 tablespoon finely chopped fresh thyme leaves, plus 1 teaspoon

1 tablespoon finely chopped fresh rosemary needles

1 teaspoon granulated garlic powder

¾ teaspoon sea salt

2 tablespoons balsamic vinegar

1½ cups Greek yogurt

1 teaspoon granulated garlic powder

TOPPING

Dijon mustard or caraway seeds, optional

Preheat the oven to 375°F. Line a rimmed baking sheet with aluminum foil.

Arrange the potatoes in a single layer on the prepared baking sheet. Toss with the olive oil, the 1 tablespoon of thyme, rosemary, garlic powder, and sea salt.

Roast for about 1 hour, or until the potatoes are tender and golden brown. Set aside to cool slightly.

Once the potatoes have cooled, transfer them to a large bowl. Add the balsamic vinegar and Greek yogurt, remaining 1 teaspoon of thyme and the garlic powder and toss gently to coat. Serve with a touch of Dijon mustard, or a sprinkle of caraway seeds.

CLEAN GREEN TIP: You know all that "low-carb, no-carb, no-starch" BS that you used to think was superrelevant? Yeah, well, not anymore. Potatoes are packed with fiber, B_6, and vitamin C. Real food is always in style.

ROASTED CURRIED
APPLE-POTATO SALAD

This antioxidant- and fiber-packed salad is a perfect side for your summer dinner and spring brunches. With the fragrant addition of caraway seeds and curry powder, you'll be in anti-inflammatory (and flavor) heaven. **Serves 4**

2 pounds red potatoes, halved and quartered
2 tablespoons extra-virgin olive oil
½ Fuji or Honeycrisp apple, halved and cut into thin slices
3 cups curly kale leaves, torn

DRESSING
3 tablespoons olive oil mayonnaise or Vegenaise mayonnaise
3 tablespoon Dijon mustard
1 tablespoon curry powder
2 tablespoons reduced-sodium tamari soy sauce or Bragg Liquid Aminos
1 tablespoon fennel or caraway seeds (optional)

Preheat the oven to 375°F and line a rimmed baking sheet with aluminum foil.

Place the potatoes on the prepared baking sheet and toss with 2 tablespoons of the olive oil to coat. Place on the middle rack in the oven and roast for 40 minutes. When the potatoes are fork-tender and crispy on the outside, remove from the oven and set aside to cool slightly.

While the potatoes are roasting, make the dressing: Whisk together the mayonnaise, mustard, curry powder, tamari soy sauce or Bragg Liquid Aminos, and caraway or fennel seeds, if using, in a large bowl until well combined.

Add the slightly cooled potatoes to the bowl and toss well to coat with the dressing. Add the apple and kale, and gently toss again and serve immediately!

ROASTED KABOCHA SQUASH SALAD

This hearty, heartwarming salad is delish as a side dish or even as a full meal. It's also a great base recipe to experiment with—feel free to swap out the quinoa with another healthy grain, like farro, freekeh, or barley. You can also swap out the kale for arugula, the apple for pear, or the pepitas for walnut or pecan pieces. Make it your own and get creative with your cooking! **Serves 6**

1 kabocha squash, halved, quartered and thinly sliced into ½-inch moons
2 tablespoons extra-virgin olive oil
¼ teaspoon sea salt
1½ cups cooked quinoa
2 cups curly kale leaves, tough stems removed, finely chopped
1 Honeycrisp or Fuji apple, cored and sliced into ¾-inch pieces
¼ cup raw pepitas

APPLE CIDER VINAIGRETTE
¼ cup plus 2 tablespoons Apple Cider Vinaigrette (page 274)

Preheat the oven to 375°F. Line a baking sheet with aluminum foil.

In a large bowl, toss the squash slices with the olive oil until well coated. Spread the squash out in an even layer across the baking sheet, making sure each piece is touching the surface of the pan to ensure even browning. Sprinkle with the sea salt. Roast in the oven for about 20 minutes, then flip the squash and roast for another 20 minutes on the opposite sides. When the squash is fork-tender, remove from the oven and set aside to cool slightly.

While the squash is roasting, make the salad: To a large bowl, add the apple cider vinaigrette, quinoa, and kale and toss gently to coat. Add the slightly cooled squash, apple slices, and pepitas to finish. Toss well to coat and serve immediately at room temperature.

POTATO-ONION BREAD

Fresh, crusty, homemade bread is just about the most delightful thing that can come out of the oven. The scent of caraway and onion mixed with the scent of freshly baked bread will fill your whole home and leave you counting the seconds until it's cool enough to cut into. **Yields one 8-inch loaf, serves 12**

1 tablespoon extra-virgin olive oil
1 small package active dry yeast
1 cup warm water
1 tablespoon honey or sugar
1½ teaspoons sea salt
1 tablespoon caraway seeds
1 small peeled potato, boiled and softly mashed (about ½ cup mashed potato)
¾ yellow onion, finely chopped and sautéed in 1 tablespoon olive oil to soften
3½ cups all-purpose flour, plus additional ½ cup for kneading

TOPPING
1 egg yolk beaten, for egg wash
½ teaspoon caraway seeds
½ teaspoon Maldon sea salt (optional)

Preheat the oven to 350°F. Lightly oil an 8-inch loaf pan with coconut oil or olive oil cooking spray, and set aside.

In a large bowl, dissolve the yeast in the warm water according to the package directions. Stir in the honey, salt, and caraway seeds.

Gently add the soft potatoes and sautéed onion, and mix with a spatula to combine. Add in 1½ cups of sifted flour, and knead into a soft dough in the bowl while continuing to add the remaining 1½ to 2 cups flour in ½-cup increments. Transfer the dough to a clean work surface sprinkled with flour, and knead well for 15 to 20 minutes, or until smooth.

Place the dough into a well-oiled bowl, cover with plastic wrap or a damp towel, and set in a warm area to rise for 40 to 50 minutes.

Form into a loaf and place into the prepared loaf pan. Brush the top of the dough with egg wash, and sprinkle with additional caraway seeds and sea salt, if desired. Bake in the oven, on the middle rack, for 30 to 40 minutes, or until fully baked and golden. Cool and slice. Serve warm with a touch of butter or olive oil.

10

CLEAN GREEN
VEGGIE
MAINS

EAT FOOD. NOT TOO MUCH.
MOSTLY PLANTS.
—Michael Pollan

CLEAN GREEN KALE-MUSHROOM LASAGNA

Researchers say you'll live a longer, happier, and healthier life if you consume less meat and more clean, plant-based protein. I say, my meatless lasagna (it can be our secret!) is a delicious way to enjoy a plant-based meal. With hearty cremini mushrooms, my rich homemade kale marinara, and ricotta cheese mix, this recipe will please the whole family. **Serves 6**

Olive oil cooking spray, for the baking dish
2 tablespoons extra-virgin olive oil
½ yellow onion, finely chopped
4 cups sliced cremini mushrooms
2 cups shredded lacinato kale leaves
2 cups part-skim ricotta cheese
3 cups Homemade Kale Marinara Sauce (page 268)
6 no-boil lasagna sheet noodles
¼ cup finely grated Pecorino Romano or Parmesan cheese

Preheat the oven to 375°F. Lightly spray a 9 x 13-inch baking dish with olive oil cooking spray and set aside.

In a large sauté pan, warm the olive oil over medium-low heat. Add the onion and cook until translucent, 6 to 8 minutes. Add the mushrooms and shredded kale, and cook for an additional 5 minutes, stirring occasionally. Remove from heat, and let cool slightly.

Place the ricotta cheese in a large bowl, and, using a spatula, gently fold in the cooled mushroom-kale mixture until completely incorporated.

ASSEMBLE THE LASAGNA

Using the prepared baking dish, assemble the lasagna in six layers as follows: 1 cup Homemade Kale Marinara, spread evenly; 3 lasagna noodle sheets (arranged in a single layer); ¾ cup of the kale-mushroom-and-ricotta mixture, spread evenly. Repeat the layering a second time, then top with the remaining kale-mushroom-and-ricotta mixture, and finish with the grated Pecorino or Romano on top. Cover with aluminum foil, and bake in the preheated oven, on the middle rack, for about 25 minutes.

After 20 minutes have passed, remove the foil from the baking dish and move the baking dish to the top rack. To finish, bake, uncovered, for another 5 to 10 minutes, depending on how you love your lasagna finished.

Remove the lasagna from the oven and cool for 5 to 10 minutes before cutting and serving.

CLEAN GREEN TIP: If you can't find no-boil lasagna noodles, you can use regular lasagna noodles, no problem. Boil them until al dente (firm to the tooth), strain, and shock with cool water, then line them up on a lightly oiled baking sheet before assembling the lasagna. That's how they do it in restaurants!

CLEAN GREEN
VEGAN LOAF

This delicious meat-less loaf was inspired by my memorable, financially challenging, book-writing times in Brooklyn. Oh, the life of a writer . . . but the great news is, there was no shortage of great food in BK. I used to visit a cozy restaurant that wasn't too pricey; they served an incredible vegan lentil loaf with oats and walnuts. I fell in love. My version will keep you happy (from all the omegas) and healthy (from all the protein and fiber) through the winter months. I still love those cheap eats and cheap thrills. **Serves 6 to 8; yields one 8-inch loaf**

Coconut oil or olive oil cooking spray, for the loaf pan
1¾ cups uncooked red lentils (yields 4 to 4½ cups cooked lentils)
5½ cups water
2 tablespoons extra-virgin olive oil
1 yellow onion, finely chopped
3 garlic cloves, minced
¼ cup tomato paste
3 cups cremini mushrooms (first measure whole, then finely chop)
3 tablespoons balsamic vinegar
3 tablespoons Bragg Liquid Aminos
¾ cup flaxseed meal
½ cup raw walnut pieces
½ cup organic rolled oats
¼ cup chopped fresh oregano, or 2 tablespoons dried

Preheat the oven to 350°F. Lightly coat an 8-inch loaf pan with coconut oil or olive oil cooking spray and set aside.

In a large stockpot, combine the lentils and water and bring to a boil. Reduce the heat and simmer for about 35 minutes, or until the lentils are a little mushy and slightly overcooked. Strain the lentils if needed. You're looking for the lentils to be soft, and not too firm—you'll be mashing them later.

In a separate large stockpot, warm the olive oil over medium-low heat. Add the onion and minced garlic and cook for about 8 minutes, or until fragrant; do not let the garlic brown. Add the tomato paste and cook for 3 minutes more, stirring with a spatula or wooden spoon. Add the chopped mushrooms and continue to cook over medium-low heat, until the liquid evaporates, 6 to 8 minutes, then turn the heat off.

Add the lentils to the pot and then fold in well. Using a potato masher, slightly mash the lentils into the mixture. Let the mixture cool slightly, then add the balsamic vinegar, Bragg Liquid Aminos, and flaxseed meal. Fold in the oats, walnut pieces, and oregano.

Transfer the mushroom-lentil mixture to the prepared loaf pan and cover with aluminum foil. Bake for 30 minutes, or until completely set and cooked through. Remove the foil, and bake for an additional 20 minutes. Remove from oven and set aside to cool.

Once the loaf is completely cool, transfer it to a clean work surface and slice it into 1½-inch pieces. Serve, topped with chutney, my Homemade Curry Ketchup (page 266), or barbecue sauce. Save the loaf in an airtight container in the fridge for up to 1 week.

CLEAN GREEN TIP: Bake the loaf mixture in mini-loaf pans or mini-muffin tins to create party-friendly bites!

JACKFRUIT CURRY TACOS

The best part about these tacos? They taste so damn good that nobody even asks what kind of protein is in them! I love swapping out the meat for jackfruit. Meet jackfruit, it is an actual fruit, native to Southeast Asia, where it is prized for its delicious flavor as well as its nutrient value. This fiber- and protein-rich fruit is full of vitamin C, potassium, and vitamin B_6. It has a slightly tropical fruit flavor that pairs perfectly here with the exotic flavors of the curry sauce. Inspire yourself to try something new! **Serves 4**

3 cups jackfruit shreds (check out Fruition brand)
½ yellow onion, finely chopped
2 tablespoons raw apple cider vinegar
2 tablespoons reduced-sodium tamari soy sauce
2 tablespoons unrefined coconut oil, melted
2 tablespoons curry powder
1 tablespoon chili powder
Coconut oil or olive oil cooking spray

GREEK YOGURT CURRY SAUCE

¼ cup Greek yogurt
1 teaspoon curry powder
1 tablespoon reduced-sodium tamari soy sauce
1 tablespoon fresh lime juice

TO ASSEMBLE

Whole-wheat or corn tortillas (warmed)
1 avocado, thinly sliced
Thinly sliced savoy cabbage

In a large nonreactive bowl or reusable container, combine the jackfruit, chopped onion, apple cider vinegar, soy sauce, coconut oil, curry powder, and chili powder. Toss well to coat. Cover the bowl or container and marinate the jackfruit for a minimum of 30 minutes, or up to 1 hour.

In a small bowl, whisk together the yogurt, curry powder, soy sauce, and lime juice. Set the sauce aside.

Add the marinated jackfruit and onion to a medium sauté pan and cook over medium heat for 8 to 10 minutes, or until fully warmed through and slightly browned.

To assemble the tacos, place a few spoonfuls of the jackfruit mixture onto the warmed tortillas and top with the yogurt curry sauce, avocado slices, and a little shredded cabbage.

ROASTED ACORN SQUASH WITH HOMEMADE KALE MARINARA

This recipe takes less time to make than it would to order in dinner, and it costs much less! Acorn squash has delicious potassium for healthy muscles, vitamin C for extra immunity, and magnesium, which may help with athletic endurance. Plus—mega bonus—it's super easy to cook. Feel free to add more basil and some chopped kale to get in even more greens (and extra flavor)! **Serves 2**

Coconut oil or olive oil cooking spray
1 acorn squash, halved, seeds removed
1 tablespoon extra-virgin olive oil
½ teaspoon sea salt
1 cup Homemade Kale Marinara Sauce (page 268)
¼ cup chiffonade of basil
2 tablespoons nutritional yeast

Preheat the oven to 350°F. Lightly coat a rimmed baking sheet with coconut oil or olive oil cooking spray.

Brush the inside of the squash with the olive oil. Sprinkle ¼ teaspoon of sea salt on each half. Place the squash halves, facedown, on the prepared baking sheet and prick several times with a fork. Bake on the middle rack of the preheated oven for about 30 minutes.

When the squash halves are soft, flip them over onto their opposite side and carefully pour ½ cup of your Homemade Kale Marinara into the cavity of each squash.

Place the squash back into the oven for another 25 minutes, or until the squash is fully cooked. You can test this by using a toothpick or a paring knife. If the inside flesh is soft, then it's done.

Remove the squash from the oven, cool slightly, and top each half with ¼ cup of basil and 2 tablespoons nutritional yeast, if using. Serve immediately.

LEMON-SOY EDAMAME BARLEY BOWL

The distinctive flavors of lemon, sesame oil, soy sauce, and oregano combine beautifully in this perfectly balanced "power lunch." I love to use fiber-rich barley as a base for hearty lunch bowls—it has such a great texture and is really filling. Add tofu, edamame, and—my favorite—avocado, and you have a totally satisfying meat-free meal. **Serves 4**

4 cups pearl or hulled barley*
4½ cups water
1½ cups shelled, organic edamame
2 cups wild baby arugula
2 blocks savory, baked, organic tofu (firm or extra-firm), cut into ¾-inch cubes
1 ripe avocado, halved and thinly sliced

LEMON TAMARI DRESSING
4 tablespoons low-sodium tamari soy sauce
2 tablespoons toasted sesame oil
Juice of 1 lemon
1 tablespoon dried oregano
1 teaspoon finely grated lemon zest (optional)

Combine the barley and water in a medium saucepan and bring to a boil. Reduce the heat to low and simmer for 40 to 50 minutes until all of the liquid is absorbed. Remove from heat and allow to cool slightly.

In a large bowl, whisk together the tamari soy sauce, sesame oil, lemon juice, oregano, and lemon zest until well combined. Add the slightly cooled barley to the bowl and toss to coat.

Add the shelled edamame and arugula and toss gently to combine. To serve, divide the barley salad among four bowls and top with tofu and avocado slices.

* Hulled barley is barley in its most natural state, which means it needs to cook for quite a bit longer than pearl barley—1 to 1½ hours longer. Pearl barley has the hull removed and is therefore less tough. Adjust your cooking time based on the variety you choose.

ROASTED SWEET POTATO AND AVOCADO BOWL WITH CARROT-GINGER VINAIGRETTE

If you want sparkling, beautiful, eyes, I'd dash to your local grocer, not the beauty supply store. No makeup, cream, or miracle salve will nourish your eyes like the vitamin A and beta-carotene you'll get from sweet potatoes and carrots! I love to curl up with this warm bowl of grains and root vegetables in the winter months. If you have any leftover roasted vegetables lying around, like squash or Brussels sprouts, they are a perfect match, so be sure to toss them in! **Serves 4**

6 cups cooked brown rice (about 3 cups uncooked)
1 cup shredded curly kale
1 cup roasted sweet potatoes, cut into 1-inch cubes
1 ripe avocado, pitted, peeled, and cubed
1 cup leftover roasted vegetables (optional)
½ cup Carrot-Ginger Vinaigrette, (page 272)

In each of four individual serving bowls, add 1½ cups brown rice. Top each with an equal amount of avocado cubes, sweet potato, shredded kale, and leftover roasted veggies, if available. Top each with 2 tablespoons of the Carrot-Ginger Vinaigrette and mix with a fork, serve at room temperature, or heat as desired. Devour and appreciate every last bite!

11

CLEAN GREEN
MEAT MAINS

THE BEST COMFORT FOOD WILL ALWAYS BE GREENS,
CORN BREAD, AND FRIED CHICKEN.
—Maya Angelou

MOM'S TORI NO KARAAGE
JAPANESE FRIED CHICKEN

Gosh, writing this recipe may have been the most nostalgic moment I've experienced in my entire career. Just the smell and taste alone is like a piece of my childhood. And I hear my mom's voice in my head as I read over her recipe and it makes me smile, every time. My mom and dad sent me an e-mail with her Japanese Fried Chicken recipe, and I draft it here with just about no modifications. This is exactly how she developed it—and it's perfect. *Domo arigato*, Mom! **Serves 4**

2 pounds fresh boneless, skinless chicken thighs (trim off excess fat)
1 cup all-purpose flour
4 to 5 cups coconut oil

MOM'S SHOYU MIX
½ cup shoyu (reduced-sodium tamari soy sauce)
2 fresh garlic cloves, grated
2 teaspoons peeled and grated fresh ginger
1 tablespoon sesame seeds

First, make Mom's Shoyu Mix: In a medium bowl, whisk together the shoyu, garlic, ginger, and sesame seeds until well combined. Place the chicken in a small airtight container and pour Mom's Shoyu Mix over the chicken. Seal the container and marinate the chicken for about 30 minutes in the refrigerator, turning chicken as needed about 15 minutes in.

Remove the chicken from the marinade, shaking off any excess liquid, and transfer to a plate.

Place the all-purpose flour on a small, clean baking sheet and coat each piece of chicken with flour, shaking off any excess.

In a large skillet or Dutch oven, heat the coconut oil over medium-high heat until the oil begins to simmer. Reduce the heat to medium; do not let the oil smoke. Cover a second small sheet pan with three layers of paper towels. Place next to the stove.

Carefully place the flour-coated chicken into the hot oil. (Mom's tip: Don't put too much chicken in at once as it will cause the temperature of the oil to drop sharply.) Cook both sides of the chicken in the oil until a beautiful brown color develops, and the chicken is cooked through. Carefully remove the chicken with tongs or a large slotted spoon, and transfer to the paper towel–lined sheet to drain excess oil.

Let cool down slightly, and get ready to enjoy the BEST chicken ever.

FUN FACTS: *Shoyu* = soy sauce; *Tori* = chicken; *Karaage* = Japanese fried chicken

ASIAN GINGER STEAK SALAD

This interchangeable meal (for hippies or weight lifters alike) can be made with marinated, grilled skirt steak or tofu . Try playing with this recipe a bit, even salmon or chicken would be delish. Toss in some thin daikon radish slices, cashews, or even some chopped Savoy cabbage for a little extra crunch. With Clean Green cooking, you can do what you want! **Serves 4**

1 pound skirt steak, or one 14-ounce package organic tofu (firm or extra-firm)*
Olive oil or coconut oil cooking spray
5 cups packed baby spinach
1 cup bean sprouts
½ cup shredded carrot
¼ red onion, thinly sliced
1 cup cooked farro or quinoa

MARINADE
3 tablespoons reduced-sodium tamari soy sauce
1 tablespoon peeled and grated fresh ginger
2 garlic cloves, grated
1 tablespoon rice vinegar
2 teaspoons manuka or raw honey

GINGER DRESSING
2 tablespoons peeled and grated fresh ginger
2 tablespoons reduced-sodium tamari soy sauce
2 tablespoons rice vinegar
2 tablespoons toasted sesame oil
2 teaspoons manuka or raw honey

First make the marinade: In a large bowl, whisk together the tamari, ginger, garlic, rice vinegar, and honey. Pour half of the marinade into a square glass baking dish, and arrange the steak or tofu on top, then pour the remaining marinade on top of the tofu or

* Make ahead of the meal. Marinate the tofu for 2 hours.

skirt steak, making sure the protein is well coated. Cover and place in the refrigerator to marinate for at least 1 hour, or up to overnight, turning the protein as needed halfway through marinating.

When the protein is fully marinated, heat a large nonstick skillet over medium heat and generously coat with coconut oil or olive oil cooking spray. Sear the steak or tofu on all four sides, 2 to 3 minutes per side. Remove from the heat and transfer the protein to a cutting board and allow to cool slightly. Using a sharp knife, slice the steak or tofu into thin slices on the diagonal. Allow the steak to rest.

In a large salad bowl, whisk together the ginger, soy sauce, rice vinegar, toasted sesame oil, and honey until well combined. To the same bowl, add the spinach, bean sprouts, carrots, red onion, and cooked grains and toss lightly to coat with the dressing.

Divide the salad among four plates or bowls, and top with the seared steak or tofu slices. Serve immediately.

KALE-MUSHROOM GYOZA

Once again, Mom inspires us all. Her gyoza in my first cookbook, *Pretty Delicious*, was clearly the fan-favorite. Well, Mom, I gave our prized family recipe a little bit of a change-up. With more shiitake mushrooms and chili flakes, and 80 percent lean ground pork, this recipe is sure to win over the whole table. **Serves 6 to 8 people as an appetizer or dinner; yields about 50 gyoza**

GYOZA

1 pound lean ground pork (80/20)

1 cup shiitake mushrooms, soaked overnight, stems removed, caps finely chopped; or 6 dried shiitake mushrooms soaked in boiling water 5 minutes, drained, and finely chopped

5 scallions, trimmed and finely chopped

1 small yellow onion, very finely chopped

1 cup finely shredded lacinato kale leaves

4 garlic cloves, minced

1/4 cup reduced-sodium tamari soy sauce

1 teaspoon crushed red chili flakes

1 teaspoon organic white sugar or coconut sugar

2 tablespoons toasted sesame oil

All-purpose flour

50 round gyoza skins (about half of a package)

2 tablespoons coconut oil, for panfrying

DIPPING SAUCE

1/4 cup reduced-sodium tamari soy sauce

1/4 cup rice vinegar

1/4 teaspoon crushed red chili flakes

1/2 scallion, thinly sliced on the diagonal

In a large bowl, using clean hands, combine the pork, mushrooms, scallions, onions, kale, and garlic. Wash your hands.

In the large bowl of pork, add the soy sauce, chili flakes, sugar, and toasted sesame oil. Mix well to combine all flavors throughout the pork.

Sprinkle a clean work surface with a handful of flour. Place a small bowl of warm water next to your work area. Set out 10 wonton wrappers on the floured area and place 2 teaspoons of the gyoza filling in the center of each. Use your fingers to moisten the edges of the wrapper with water and then fold the wrapper over the filling (as if you were making a turnover) and press the edges together to seal. Set aside and repeat with the rest of the filling and wrappers.

Heat 1½ teaspoons of the coconut oil in a large nonstick skillet over medium-high heat for 2 minutes. Add about 10 gyoza to the skillet, seam side up. (They should have some elbow room so you can flip them easily.) Cook until the bottoms are golden brown, 1 to 2 minutes. (When peeking under the gyoza to check the color, be gentle—they are fragile!) Add ¼ cup of water to the skillet to release the gyoza from the pan, lower the heat to medium, and cover. Cook until the wrappers are translucent, about 2 minutes. Remove the lid and cook until the water has evaporated and the filling is cooked through, 2 to 3 minutes more, as needed.

When the gyoza are done, turn off the heat, remove the lid, and pour off the oil from the pan into a bowl. Set aside for the next batch. Place a large plate over the skillet (the plate should be larger than the skillet) and flip the pan over—the gyoza should effortlessly fall from the skillet onto the plate revealing their gorgeous golden-brown skins. Gyoza taste best when hot, so serve immediately with the dipping sauce as you cook up the next batch.

Cook 5 more batches, adding a tiny bit more oil as needed and ¼ cup water for each batch. Wipe out the skillet between batches if necessary.

To make your dipping sauce: In a small dish, whisk the soy sauce and vinegar together. Add the chili flakes and scallions. Serve up and dip! *Itedakimasu!*

CLEAN GREEN TIP: Gyoza, a traditional Japanese dumpling, is an absolute favorite in Japan. You'll find this delicious, juicy, and crisp staple appetizer/meal at every quality Japanese restaurant and household. Traditionally they are made with pork, but you can swap in beef, chicken, or shrimp, or even a soft cashew mix, if you prefer.

MISO-ORANGE
GLAZED SALMON

Want to build a better brain? Eat more wild salmon! Packed with omega-3 fatty acids, salmon is one of the healthiest, mega-brain-boosting foods you can eat. I love the combination of citrus and miso with salmon. This recipe is super easy to throw together and really shows off the flavor of the fish—so always purchase the freshest, best-quality wild fish you can find! **Serves 4**

MARINADE

Coconut oil or olive oil cooking spray, for the baking dish

2 tablespoons miso paste

2 tablespoons rice vinegar

3 tablespoons fresh orange juice, preferably from a whole orange

3 teaspoons finely grated orange zest

2 teaspoons toasted sesame oil

1 tablespoon reduced-sodium tamari soy sauce

Four 5-ounce, 1-inch-thick salmon fillets, skin on

1 tablespoon toasted sesame seeds, for garnish

2 scallions, trimmed and thinly sliced on the diagonal, for garnish

Cooked brown rice or sautéed greens, for serving

Preheat the oven to 350°F. Lightly coat a 9 x 13-inch baking dish with coconut oil or olive oil cooking spray and set aside.

In a medium bowl, whisk together the miso paste, rice vinegar, orange juice, 2 teaspoons of the orange zest, toasted sesame oil, and tamari soy sauce for the marinade.

Place the salmon fillets, skin side down, in a shallow dish or resealable container and brush with about half of the marinade. Cover and place in the refrigerator to marinate for about 20 minutes.

Remove the salmon from the refrigerator and brush with the rest of the marinade. Transfer to the prepared baking dish and bake until the salmon is opaque at the edges and the center is still pink, 15 to 20 minutes. Remove from the oven and cool for 5 minutes.

Sprinkle with the sesame seeds, scallions, and the remaining 1 teaspoon orange zest. Serve with brown rice and/or sautéed greens.

CLEAN GREEN TIP: Welcome a fab new word to your diet: koji. Koji is the result of combining cooked rice or soybeans with a natural fermentation culture, which breaks down protein and carbohydrates from the beans or rice into amino acids. Koji is the base commonly used to make some of your favorites, like sake, miso, and soy sauce.

Koji is also packed with heart-protecting isoflavones—powerful free radical–fighting antioxidants that can keep your bones strong. Fun fact: one of the amino acids created by this process, glutamate, creates a delish and unique umami-like flavor.

CHILI-LIME SHRIMP TOSTADAS

These seriously craveable tostadas are packed with feel-good ingredients that also offer nutritional benefits: shrimp for clean protein and zinc, kale for immunity-boosting and antioxidant-packed vitamins A, C, K, and garlic for manganese and selenium. It is simple, delicious, and oh so good for you. **Serves 4 as an appetizer; 2 as a main course**

TOSTADA CRISPS

Coconut oil or olive oil cooking spray

4 small corn tortillas, about 6 inches (you can also purchase small tostadas if available)

1 tablespoon extra-virgin olive oil, plus 2 teaspoons

½ teaspoon sea salt

1 pound large (16/20) uncooked, peeled, and deveined shrimp, tails removed

CHILI-LIME SHRIMP MARINADE

2 tablespoons reduced-sodium tamari soy sauce

1 tablespoon fresh lime juice

1 teaspoon crushed red chili flakes

2 tablespoons minced fresh garlic

TOPPING

1 cup wild arugula or finely chopped lacinato kale leaves

1 ripe avocado, thinly sliced

2 tablespoons fresh cilantro, finely chopped

¼ cup Cotija or queso fresco cheese (optional)

1 lime, cut into wedges

Preheat the oven to 350°F. Line a rimmed baking sheet with aluminum foil and lightly coat with coconut oil or olive oil cooking spray.

Arrange the corn tortillas on the baking sheet, brush with 2 teaspoons of the olive oil, and sprinkle with sea salt. Bake in the oven for 25 minutes, or until all the tortillas are crisp and golden. Remove from the oven and set aside to cool.

Rinse the shrimp with cool water, and pat dry with paper towels.

In a medium resealable container, whisk together the tamari soy sauce, lime juice, chili flakes, and minced garlic until well combined. Add the shrimp and toss gently to coat. Cover the container and transfer to the refrigerator to marinate the shrimp for about 20 minutes, turning as needed halfway after about 10 minutes.

Remove the shrimp from the marinade. Heat the 1 tablespoon of olive oil in a large sauté pan over medium heat. When the oil is hot, add the shrimp and sauté, turning occasionally, until cooked through, about 5 minutes. Reserve the pan sauce.

Arrange the shrimp on each tostada crisp. Top with the arugula or shredded kale, avocado slices, cilantro, Cotija cheese (if using), a spoonful of the reserved pan sauce, and a squeeze of fresh lime juice. Serve immediately.

OKONOMIYAKI
SAVORY PANCAKES

During an incredible, life-changing trip to Tokyo, Kyoto, Hiroshima, and
Beppu (my mom's hometown), I tested about ten different okonomiyaki recipes.
Okonomiyaki are savory Japanese pancakes that can be topped with everything
from eggs and bacon to oysters and ramen. There was one that particularly
stood out in Hiroshima. I had learned that okonomiyaki was "a food of war,"
created because there was very little food available during World War II; the
women created okonomiyaki stands to support their families and to make ends
meet. With ingredients like cabbage, flour, and water, they cooked to support
and survive. Every time I make this recipe, I think of them, and the strength
and history of Japan. It's incredible how war can create recipes of necessity that
continue for generations. **Serves 6; yields 6 pancakes**

2 cups all-purpose flour

1¾ cups cold water

1 teaspoon peeled and grated fresh ginger

3 tablespoons reduced-sodium tamari soy sauce

3 scallions, finely diced

¾ cup cabbage, finely chopped

Toasted sesame seed oil, for panfrying the pancakes

TOPPINGS (ALL OPTIONAL)

Smoked fish, trout, or salmon, broken or flaked with a fork

Savory baked organic tofu (firm or extra-firm), crumbled

Bacon slices

Tamago (whole egg)

Furikake (toasted seaweed and sesame seasoning)

Shredded cabbage

Negi (scallions)

Bean sprouts

In a large bowl, whisk together the flour, cold water, grated ginger, and tamari soy sauce. Fold in the finely chopped scallions and cabbage. The consistency should resemble crepe batter.

In a medium nonstick sauté pan over medium heat, add a touch of toasted sesame oil. Ladle about ¼ cup of the batter into a round crepe shape, cook for 1 to 2 minutes on the first side, then flip using a stiff spatula. Cook for another 1 to 2 minutes on the opposite side.

Meanwhile, add your choice of toppings in a single flat layer. Example: shredded cabbage, crumbled savory tofu, katsuobushi (bonito flakes), furikake (toasted seaweed and sesame seasoning), etc. Drizzle 1½ tablespoons of the batter on top of your toppings and, using a spatula, carefully flip the pancake again to cook the toppings for another 1 to 2 minutes. Remove from the pan and add your favorite sauces and toppings to finish.

OKAASAN'S (MOM'S) TIPS:

- *Okonimi* means "as you wish, as you like."
- Use toasted sesame oil, *gomabura*, to cook the okonomiyaki with rich flavor.
- Try Japanese Kewpi mayonnaise (like the best thing ever) to top.
- Dried bonito flakes (katsuobushi) add more flavor.
- The Japanese love their *beni shoga*, aka "pickled ginger," to top their okonomiyaki! YUM!

BROWN RICE SUSHI ROLLS

SUSHI! A staple in our household growing up, of course my mom still makes the absolute best! I wanted to share this delicious recipe with you and your families, so you can see how simple it can be to make at home. I swapped out white rice in place for brown here, as I wanted to boost the fiber and protein value. Roll away . . . ! **Serves 4 as an appetizer; 2 for a meal**

SUSHI SUPPLIES

Bamboo mat
Rice paddle
Paper fan
Sharp knife
Clean, wet towel

10 to 12 sheets toasted nori (seaweed)
About 3 cups cooked brown rice

SUSHI-SU (SUSHI VINEGAR)

3 tablespoons rice vinegar
3 tablespoons organic sugar
1 teaspoon salt

OPTIONAL FILLERS

1 ripe avocado, thinly sliced
Fresh basil leaves
1 cucumber, thinly sliced lengthwise
Carrots, thinly sliced
Japanese kaiware sprouts
Japanese umeboshi plums, discard seeds
Daikon pickles or fresh daikon

OPTIONAL PROTEINS

Crabmeat
Smoked salmon, thinly sliced
Savory baked organic tofu (firm or extra-firm), thinly sliced

Furikake (Japanese Mrs. Dash)

Toasted sesame seeds

Togarashi spice (see page 23)

Sriracha hot sauce

Ponzu sauce, for dipping

Reduced-sodium tamari soy sauce and wasabi, for dipping

Make your sushi rice. Cook the brown rice as directed on the package (roughly 2 parts rice: 1 part water). Cool the rice slightly while preparing your *sushi-su* (sushi vinegar).

In a medium bowl, whisk together the rice vinegar, sugar, and sea salt until the sugar and salt have dissolved.

Transfer the slightly cooled rice to a large bowl. Using a rice paddle and a small paper fan, fan the rice as you slowly drizzle the vinegar mixture over it. Cut the rice with the rice paddle, as you fan the rice to cool, using a hand fan or just a magazine. Be sure not to mix the rice. Simply cut through the rice until all of the vinegar has been absorbed.

While the rice is still warm, roll your sushi. Prep a clean work surface, like a clean cutting board or a clean countertop. Lay down your bamboo mat on the work surface. Place the nori on top of the bamboo mat, shiny side down, matte side up.

Using your rice paddle, spread a layer of about ½ cup sushi rice in the middle of the nori sheet. At the bottom of the sushi roll closest to you, add your choice of fillers, proteins, and seasonings in a horizontal line. Tightly roll, from the bottom up, into a long *maki* roll. Gently squeeze the bamboo mat to tighten your roll.

Remove the bamboo mat, and cut the roll in half. (Wipe off the knife with a clean towel in between slices.) Next, line up your two halves and cut into fourths and sixths. Repeat making rolls until all the rice is used. Serve the rolls immediately with your favorite sauces.

PORK RAMEN

When I was growing up my mom made sure we drove a few hours from San Diego to Los Angeles to get simply the best pork ramen. This recipe took me months to perfect (I even enlisted the help of my ramen-master friend Kenshiro) and I think it will do the trick . . . for now . . . but I will always go back to Kyushu, Japan, for the real thing!

Note: This is a slow-cooked recipe, so be sure to start cooking midday before dinner. **Serves 4**

2 tablespoons toasted sesame oil (gomabura)
1 yellow onion, halved and thinly sliced
4 garlic cloves, crushed
2 pounds pork ribs, cut into 1- to 2-rib portions
10 cups cold water
2 teaspoons sea salt
4 packages ramen noodles, fresh ramen noodles are best!
    (Look for Sun brand fresh ramen)

TARE
¼ cup mirin (Japanese rice wine vinegar)
¼ cup reduced-sodium tamari soy sauce
¼ cup high-quality sake
2 small pieces kombu (Japanese seaweed),
    broken to fit in pan
1 tablespoon brown sugar
2 garlic cloves, crushed

TOPPING (OPTIONAL)
Reserved and slow-cooked pork meat (see below for cooking method)
Hard-boiled eggs, halved
Chopped kale
Wild arugula
Watercress
Pickled ginger (beni shoga, gari shoga)
Scallions, cut on the diagonal

Bean sprouts

Furikake

Hot chili oil

Togarashi

White pepper

Gobo root cut on the diagonal

Crisp bacon slices

Enoki mushrooms

Nori pieces

To a large stockpot over medium heat, add the toasted sesame oil and the onion and cook until softened, about 5 minutes. Add the garlic and stir until fragrant, about 3 minutes more. Add the pork ribs and stir to coat the ribs with the onions and garlic. Reduce the heat to medium-low and begin to brown all sides of the ribs, using tongs to rotate the ribs occasionally.

When pork ribs are slightly browned on all sides, add 10 cups of cold water and the sea salt to the pot, making sure that all the ribs are covered. Bring the water up to a light simmer. Simmer on low heat, uncovered, for about 5 hours.

While the stock is cooking, make the tare (this is a ramen soup base). In a medium saucepan over medium-low heat, combine the mirin, soy sauce, sake, kombu, brown sugar, and garlic cloves. Cook, stirring occasionally until reduced to nappé consistency (coats the back of a spoon), about 15 minutes. Set aside to cool.

When the stock is ready, strain it twice through a fine-mesh strainer, reserving the stock. Cool slightly, reserve the meat, and discard the bones.

Cook the ramen noodles in boiling water for about 3 minutes, strain and shock with cold water. Do not plate up until you are ready to eat, as ramen noodles soak up liquid quickly!

When ready to plate, place 1 tablespoon of the tare into each of four bowls, ladle in 1 cup of the pork stock, and finish with one-fourth of the noodles. Top with the pork and your choice of hard-boiled egg, bacon slices, extra pork, scallions, or anything else you want. Finish with a dash of white pepper, togarashi spice, or chili oil.

CLEAN GREEN TIP: Ramen is meant to be quick, delicious, and simple, but not "to-go." Some authentic ramen joints in NYC won't even do takeout because it compromises the integrity of the noodles. The broth can take months to mature and perfect. The noodles must be consumed right after the broth is added, and the tare/soup base has got to be just right. So next time you're thinking ramen, remember how prized this real Japanese indulgence is. It should never be "instant"!

KALE FRIED RICE

Leftover grains are, hands down, the best staple to have on hand to create some masterpiece recipes. This simple and delicious one-pan fried rice is a perfect full meal to make in minutes. Feel free to throw in any leftover protein you may have in the fridge—this pairs well with anything from chicken to beef to salmon!

Serves 4

2 cups freekeh or farro or 4 cups leftover grains
2 tablespoons toasted sesame oil
2 tablespoons reduced-sodium tamari soy sauce
1 yellow onion, finely diced
1 garlic clove, minced
3 carrots, peeled and thinly sliced on the diagonal
5 scallions thinly sliced on the diagonal
2 eggs, beaten (we found these eggs shot here on the farm!)
1 medium sausage (like kielbasa or chicken sausage) cooked through
    and sliced on the diagonal (omit if serving a vegetarian dish and
    substitute with crumbled tofu)
1 cup finely shredded kale leaves

In a medium saucepan, bring 2 cups uncooked farro or freekeh and 4 to 5 cups water to a boil, then reduce to a simmer. Simmer for 25 to 30 minutes until tender. Drain any excess liquid, fluff with a fork, and set aside to cool.

Place a large nonstick skillet or wok over medium-high heat. Add the toasted sesame oil, soy sauce, onion, and garlic and stir-fry for about 3 minutes. Add the carrots and scallions and stir-fry for another 3 minutes, or until thoroughly heated.

Reduce the heat to low, create a well in the center of the skillet using a rubber spatula, and add the beaten eggs, stirring gently, to form soft scrambled eggs. Add the sausage or tofu and your choice of grains and sauté until warmed through. Add the chopped kale and toss gently to coat and quickly warm through. Top with remaining scallions or even some sesame seeds and serve immediately.

SPICY SHRIMP SOBA
NOODLE SALAD

This fiery dish is definitely a metabolism booster and a delightful full-meal salad as I've found that everyone loves soba noodles. Be sure to watch the heat on this recipe, as it is a little on the spicy side. If you like it hot, this one's for you! **Serves 6**

1 pound medium (41/50) uncooked shrimp, thawed, peeled, and deveined, tails removed
One 8-ounce package soba, cooked, cooled, and drained
1 cup organic edamame (if using frozen, thawed)
1 cup fresh baby arugula
2 scallions, finely sliced on the diagonal

MARINADE

2 tablespoons rice vinegar
2 tablespoons reduced-sodium tamari soy sauce
1 teaspoon maple syrup or honey
¼ to ½ teaspoon cayenne pepper
1 teaspoon peeled and grated fresh ginger
1 tablespoon toasted sesame oil (gomabura)

DRESSING

2½ tablespoons reduced-sodium tamari soy sauce
¼ tablespoons plus 2 tablespoons rice vinegar
1 tablespoon toasted sesame seed oil (gomabura)
¼ to ½ teaspoon cayenne pepper

TOPPING

2 tablespoons whole fresh mint leaves
2 tablespoons fresh cilantro leaves (optional)
1 tablespoon toasted sesame seeds

Rinse the shrimp under cool water and pat dry with paper towels.

In a medium nonreactive container, make the marinade. Whisk together the rice vinegar, soy sauce, maple syrup or honey, cayenne, and grated ginger until the marinade is well combined. Add the shrimp and toss gently to coat. Cover the container and place in the refrigerator to marinate for about 20 minutes, turning as needed after 10 minutes.

Remove the shrimp from the fridge. Place a large sauté pan over medium-high heat, add the marinated shrimp to the hot pan, and sauté until cooked through, about 5 minutes. Remove the shrimp from heat and set aside.

In a large bowl, whisk together the ingredients for the dressing. Gently add the cooked and cooled soba noodles and edamame and toss well to coat with the dressing. Mix in the arugula and scallions. Top with mint leaves, cilantro (if using), toasted sesame seeds, and shrimp. Enjoy immediately, and even a few days later—this salad holds fabulously well overnight in the fridge!

Pasta with Sun-Dried Tomato Pesto

12

CLEAN GREEN
PIZZAS AND
PASTAS

I AM A GLUTTON. I'LL EAT WHATEVER IS THERE. PIZZA.
I'VE GOT NOTHING AGAINST ANY OF THAT. IF I FEEL LIKE
EATING, I EAT. I DON'T FEEL GUILTY ABOUT IT AT ALL.
—Jacques Pépin

CAPRESE PIZZA

Fresh, thinly sliced heirloom tomatoes, farm-fresh basil, and Homemade Kale Marinara Sauce make up this delightful and deliciously fresh-tasting pizza. I made sure to focus on ingredients that give back to you. Enjoy and appreciate every bite of this clean green Caprese! **Serves 4**

All-purpose flour, for rolling the dough
1 pound store-bought regular or gluten-free pizza dough
2 teaspoons extra-virgin olive oil
1/8 teaspoon sea salt
1/3 cup Homemade Kale Marinara Sauce (see page 268)
Four to five 1/4-inch rounds, fresh mozzarella cheese
3 medium heirloom tomatoes, thinly sliced into 1/4-inch rounds
1/2 cup basil leaves, torn, to finish
Maldon sea salt, for finishing (optional)

Preheat the oven to 400°F. Place both oven racks in the middle position. Remove the pizza dough from the fridge and let it come to room temperature for 20 minutes.

Sprinkle a clean work surface with flour, and roll out the dough into a flat circle 1/4 inch thick and place into a cast-iron skillet or on a pizza stone. Brush the dough with the olive oil and sprinkle with sea salt.

Spread the marinara sauce evenly on the pizza, leaving about a 1-inch border around the outer edge of the crust. Top with the thinly sliced mozzarella and tomato slices. Bake the pizza on the middle rack for about 25 minutes, or until the sides are golden and crisp to the touch. The tomatoes will release some liquid, so simply use a paper towel to dab and soak up the pizza.

Remove the pizza from the oven, allow the cheese to melt for 2 to 4 minutes, and finish with fresh basil and sea salt, if using.

CLEAN GREEN TIP: Love pesto like crazy? Swap out the marinara sauce for my kale pesto (see page 236) and get your extra greens on. Remember to use sparingly—a little pesto goes a long way!

SWEET POTATO PIZZA

Like seriously FABULOUS! This recipe was originally developed as an idea for Thanksgiving leftovers. It dawned on me that sweet potato mash on a pizza with leftover roasted vegetables might be the best thing ever. And it was! This recipe is a constant reminder that creativity is key and there are no rules in cooking.

Serves 6

2 cups unpeeled sweet potatoes (roughly 2 medium sweet potatoes),
    cut into 2-inch cubes (or use leftover sweet potato mash!)
3 tablespoons extra-virgin olive oil, plus 2 teaspoons, divided
2 cups roasted asparagus, cut into ½-inch pieces on the diagonal,
    or any leftover roasted vegetables you have on hand
1 tablespoon balsamic vinegar
½ teaspoon sea salt
1 pound store-bought regular or gluten-free pizza dough
All-purpose flour, for rolling the dough
Coconut oil or olive oil cooking spray
¼ teaspoon sea salt

TOPPING
1 cup watercress greens
1 cup wild baby arugula
2 teaspoons extra-virgin olive oil
2 teaspoons balsamic vinegar
2 tablespoons grated Parmesan or Pecorino cheese (or try vegan cheese as an option!)

Preheat the oven to 400°F. Place both oven racks in the middle position. Line two rimmed baking sheets with aluminum foil.

Place the sweet potatoes on one baking sheet and coat with 1 tablespoon of the olive oil.

Place the asparagus on the second baking sheet and coat with 1 tablespoon of the olive oil and the balsamic vinegar. Place both baking sheets in the oven. After 25 minutes, remove the sheet with asparagus and set aside. Let the potatoes roast for an additional 20 minutes, or until tender. Remove the pizza dough from the fridge and let it come to room temperature.

When the sweet potatoes are finished roasting, carefully place into a large food processor. Add the remaining 1 tablespoon olive oil and pulse to create a thick sweet potato purée.

To roll the room-temperature pizza dough, lightly grease a pizza stone or round cast-iron skillet with coconut oil or olive oil cooking spray. On a clean, flat, flour-dusted work surface, roll out the dough into a 12- to 13-inch round, ½ inch thick. Transfer the dough to the prepared baking sheet.

Brush the dough with the 2 teaspoons olive oil, and sprinkle the dough with the sea salt. Using the back of a large spoon, spread the sweet potato mash on as the base, as you would with a sauce, then top with the roasted asparagus.

Bake the pizza in the oven on the middle rack for about 25 minutes until the sides are golden and crisp to the touch. Remove from oven.

In a small bowl, lightly toss the watercress and arugula with the olive oil and balsamic vinegar. Finish topping the pizza with the dressed greens and freshly grated Parmesan cheese.

KALE-BACON PIZZA

(LS)

This happy recipe was created by my man and me for at-home movie nights. Make the pizza, pop it into the oven, watch your movie for just a bit, and enjoy this delish pizza when it comes out of the oven. No need for takeout anymore, as the bacon-fat-coated kale and cracked egg will have you hooked on making your own pizza at home! **Serves 4 to 6**

3 slices organic bacon, cut into 1-inch pieces
½ yellow onion, finely diced
2 cups kale, tough ribs and stems removed, leaves finely chopped
All-purpose flour, for rolling the dough
1 pound store-bought pizza dough (gluten-free pizza dough is great!)
2 teaspoons extra-virgin olive oil
¼ teaspoon sea salt, plus more as desired
⅓ cup organic marinara sauce or Homemade Kale Marinara Sauce (page 268)
4 ounces mozzarella cheese (fresh or shredded, your choice)

Preheat the oven to 400°F. Set the pizza dough out to at room temperature for about 20 minutes.

In a large skillet over medium heat, cook the bacon until crisp, about 5 minutes. Set the bacon aside on paper towels and reserve the bacon fat in the skillet. Add the diced onion to the bacon fat and cook over medium heat, stirring occasionally, until softened, about 8 minutes. Add the chopped kale and cook until wilted, about 2 minutes. Set the skillet aside.

On a clean work surface, dusted with a touch of flour and using clean hands, roll out the pizza dough into a 10- to 12-inch round, ½ to ¾ inch thick. Lightly grease a large baking sheet, pizza stone, or a round cast-iron skillet. Place the dough on the baking sheet (or in the skillet/on the stone), brush with olive oil, and sprinkle with sea salt.

Prebake the crust in the oven for about 10 minutes, until slightly puffed. Remove the crust from the oven and top with the marinara sauce, mozzarella, kale-onion mixture, and bacon. Bake on the middle rack for about 15 minutes. Remove from the oven and sprinkle with the additional sea salt to finish, if desired. Serve immediately with a glass of Pinot!

SPAGHETTI AND KALE-MUSHROOM BOLOGNESE

When you're remaking classic recipes, it's important not to compromise the integrity of a beloved dish. The main difference between this spaghetti and the traditional Bolognese we all love is the addition of kale. I'm a huge fan of pairing lean ground meats with flavorful veggies like kale, mushrooms, onions, and fresh herbs. This delicious and "green" pasta dish is one of my favorites. **Serves 6**

2 tablespoons extra-virgin olive oil

1 yellow onion, finely diced

2 celery stalks, finely diced

2 carrots, peeled, finely diced

1 cup cremini mushrooms, finely diced

2 tablespoons tomato paste

¼ cup fabulous red wine (Cabernet works perfectly)

1 pound 80 percent lean ground beef

One 28-ounce can organic crushed tomatoes

1 teaspoon sea salt

1 cup finely chopped kale leaves

One 14.5- to 16- ounce box whole-wheat or gluten-free spaghetti

TOPPING

¼ cup grated Parmesan cheese or nutritional yeast (optional)

¼ cup fresh basil leaves (optional)

In a large stockpot over medium heat, warm the olive oil. Add the onion and cook for about 5 minutes, or until soft. Add the celery and carrot and cook for an additional 5 minutes. Add the mushrooms and cook for 5 minutes more, or until all the liquid has evaporated.

Add the tomato paste, and stir to coat all the vegetables. Sauté for an additional 5 minutes to deepen and develop the flavor. Add the meat, stirring frequently with a wooden spoon to break up any large pieces, and sauté for about 10 minutes, until the meat is cooked through.

Increase the heat to medium-high, add the red wine, and deglaze the pan. Cook until all the alcohol has evaporated and the brown bits have released from the bottom of the pan, 2 to 3 minutes.

Add the crushed tomatoes and the sea salt. Reduce the heat to low, and cook for 35 minutes, stirring occasionally.

While the sauce reduces, cook the pasta in a large stockpot to just al dente. Shock with cold water to stop cooking and set aside.

To serve, add the cooked and cooled pasta to the pot of sauce and toss to coat the pasta well. Spoon into individual bowls and top with the Parmesan cheese, if using, and fresh basil.

CLEAN GREEN SPINACH GNOCCHI
WITH LEMON BUTTER SAUCE

This simple and delicious method for making the perfect gnocchi was inspired by my friend Chef Marco Canora, who always says that simple techniques combined with good-quality ingredients make for the best food. A potato ricer or food mill is a great way to get perfectly fluffy potatoes, but if you don't have one, you can also use a fine-mesh strainer. Just push the potato through it and then fluff with a fork.

Serves 2

1 large Yukon Gold potato, peeled and cut into 1-inch cubes

RICOTTA CREAM MIXTURE
3 tablespoons part-skim ricotta cheese
1 cup baby spinach, packed
2 tablespoons fresh basil leaves
¼ teaspoon sea salt
¾ cup all-purpose flour, plus extra for shaping

LEMON BUTTER SAUCE
2 tablespoons unsalted butter
2 teaspoons finely grated lemon zest
¼ teaspoon sea salt

Fill a medium saucepan halfway with water and place over high heat. When the water boils, add the potato cubes and reduce to a simmer. Cook for about 10 minutes, or until the potato cubes are fork-tender. Drain and set the potatoes aside to cool on paper towels to ensure that all the excess water is removed. When the potatoes have cooled slightly, run them through a potato ricer.

Place the ricotta, spinach, basil, and salt into a food processor or blender and pulse for 20 to 30 seconds until combined. Transfer the mixture to a medium bowl.

Liberally flour a clean work surface, transfer the potatoes to the surface. Add the ricotta mixture to the potatoes and begin to dust with a light coat of flour across the top. Using clean hands, gently combine the ingredients into a round of dough, and continue sprinkling flour as needed until all the ingredients are incorporated. Take extra care not

to overmix, or the potatoes will get gluey! Gently form the gnocchi dough into a disk. Divide the disk into 3 equal pieces.

In the meantime, bring a medium pot of salted water to a boil. Flour a rimmed baking sheet.

Using a dough scraper, clean your work surface. Flour your hands and roll all three pieces of dough into ¾- to 1-inch-wide rope. Using a pizza cutter or a sharp knife, slice the rope crosswise into ¾-inch-wide pillows. Transfer the gnocchi to the floured baking sheet and repeat rolling and continue to slice the remaining dough.

When the water has come to a gentle boil, carefully add the gnocchi, in batches, and cook until the gnocchi float to the surface, 2 to 4 minutes total. While the gnocchi are cooking, prepare the lemon butter sauce.

In a small saucepan over medium heat, combine the butter, lemon zest, and sea salt. When butter has melted, using a slotted spoon, transfer the cooked gnocchi to the sauce and toss well to coat. Repeat with the remaining gnocchi. Serve immediately while hot!

CREAMY BUTTERNUT SQUASH AND SHELLS

Once you make this there's no turning back: your new go-to mac and cheese recipe. With creamy, velvety butternut squash and decadent, rich coconut milk, there's a new way to indulge in mac and cheese! I love using shells or penne in my mac and cheese, but feel free to use elbow macaroni or whatever pasta you'd like—you could also swap in whole-wheat or gluten-free pasta. **Serves 8**

1 medium butternut squash, peeled, halved, seeded,
　and chopped into 1-inch cubes
2 garlic cloves, finely chopped
2 sprigs fresh thyme
1/2 teaspoon freshly grated nutmeg
3/4 teaspoon sea salt
1 cup low-sodium vegetable broth
1 1/2 cups canned light coconut milk
4 cups pasta shells or penne, cooked and drained (your choice, gluten-free or regular
　pasta!)
1/4 cup plus 2 tablespoons Gruyère, Parmesan, or nutritional yeast
Coconut oil or olive oil cooking spray, for the pan

HERBED BREAD-CRUMB TOPPING
1/2 cup panko bread crumbs
1 tablespoon granulated garlic powder
1/4 teaspoon sea salt
1/2 cup finely chopped kale leaves

Preheat the oven to 375°F. Lightly coat a 9 x 13-inch pan with coconut oil or olive oil cooking spray.

In a large saucepan, combine the butternut squash, garlic cloves, thyme sprigs, nutmeg, salt, broth, and coconut milk. Cook over medium heat, uncovered, stirring occasionally and making sure that all the squash is submerged. Simmer until the butternut squash is fork-tender, about 30 minutes. Remove and discard the thyme sprigs.

Carefully place the squash mixture in a food processor or blender and purée until velvety smooth.

Meanwhile, cook the pasta in salted water until al dente. Drain and rinse with cool water, remove all excess liquid.

Spread out the pasta in the prepared pan, and pour the squash–coconut milk purée over the pasta. Gently fold in the ¼ cup cheese and mix well to combine, ensuring that all noodles are coated. Cover the dish with aluminum foil and place in preheated oven. Bake for about 30 minutes, or until bubbly and cooked through.

Meanwhile, in a small bowl, combine the ingredients for the topping.

Remove the mac and cheese from the oven, uncover, and sprinkle the top with the herbed bread-crumb topping, followed by a sprinkle of the remaining 2 tablespoons grated cheese or nutritional yeast. Transfer to the broiler for 2 to 3 minutes until brown and bubbly. Remove, cool slightly, and serve!

PASTA WITH SUN-DRIED TOMATO PESTO

Once you see how simple and delicious it is to whip up fresh, clean pesto at home, you'll never go back to store-bought, jarred, oily, oxidized pesto again! This clean and nutritious pesto, full of vitamins A, C, E, and antioxidants, combines the traditional ingredients of garlic, olive oil, salt, and basil with raw almonds for a creamy, nutty, and protein-packed sauce. **Serves 6; yields 1½ cups pesto**

SUN-DRIED TOMATO PESTO

¾ cup whole raw almonds

3 cups fresh basil leaves, stems removed

3 garlic cloves, roughly chopped

¼ cup oil-packed sun-dried tomatoes
   (measure oil-packed tomatoes with minimal oil)

½ teaspoon sea salt

⅓ cup extra-virgin olive oil

¼ cup water

2 tablespoons fresh lemon juice

PASTA

1½ cups penne or bow-tie pasta (whole wheat or gluten free)

TOPPING

1 to 2 tablespoons thinly shaved Parmesan cheese (optional)

Place the almonds into a food processor and pulse until ground. Add the basil, garlic, sun-dried tomatoes, and sea salt and pulse again to combine. Once the ingredients are somewhat mealy, gradually add the olive oil and water, and process until the mixture is finely chopped yet still has texture, about 1 minute. Pulse in the lemon juice.

Begin to cook your pasta. When it's al dente (firm to the tooth), strain and cool. Place the warm pasta into a large bowl, and toss with ⅓ cup pesto until well coated. Top with fresh basil and Parmesan, if desired.

CLEAN GREEN TIP: I love to keep extra pesto on hand in my freezer. To store your pesto, you can use a freezer-friendly container or zip-top bag, or pour the pesto into a clean ice cube tray so you can pop out a serving as needed. You will thank yourself on a busy weeknight, or the next time unexpected company shows up for dinner!

ROASTED SPAGHETTI SQUASH AND KALE PESTO

This is the perfect dish for a chilly night. Make your kale pesto in advance and you can whip up this comforting and impressive "pasta" dish in minutes. You can also swap in the Sun-Dried Tomato Pesto (page 235) or Homemade Kale Marinara Sauce (page 268) if you happen to have either of those clean green sauces on hand!

Serves 4 as a side dish; 2 as a main course

Coconut oil or olive oil cooking spray, for the baking sheet
1 large spaghetti squash, cut in half lengthwise (approx. 1½ to 2 pounds)
1 tablespoon extra-virgin olive oil to oil the squash prior to roasting
½ teaspoon sea salt
2 tablespoons grated Parmesan cheese or nutritional yeast (optional)
¼ cup fresh basil leaves (optional)

KALE PESTO
Makes ¾ cup pesto
1½ cups lacinato kale leaves, torn
½ cup whole, raw almonds
1 to 2 garlic cloves
¼ teaspoon sea salt
1 tablespoon fresh lemon juice
3 tablespoons extra-virgin olive oil

Preheat the oven to 350°F. Lightly coat a rimmed baking sheet with coconut oil or olive oil cooking spray.

Using a spoon, scoop out the pulp and seeds from the inside of the squash. Drizzle both halves with olive oil and rub to coat. Sprinkle with sea salt to taste.

Place the squash halves, cut side down, on the prepared baking sheet and roast for about 45 minutes. Carefully flip each half over and roast for another 10 minutes, or until fork-tender. Remove the squash from the oven and allow it to cool slightly.

While the squash cools, make the kale pesto: In a food processor, add the kale, almonds, garlic, salt, and lemon juice. Pulse until coarsely chopped. Stream in the olive oil and process until a smooth paste forms.

Using a fork, fluff up the strands of "spaghetti" from the inside of the squash. Magic! Lightly coat each half of the roasted squash with ¼ cup of the kale pesto, and add a sprinkle of Parmesan or fresh basil on top, if desired. Serve just as you would pasta, adding more or less fresh pesto or basil as desired. Leftover pesto will keep in the freezer for up to 3 months.

13

CLEAN GREEN SWEETS AND TREATS

A PARTY WITHOUT CAKE IS REALLY JUST A MEETING.
—Julia Child

COCONUT-DATE BITES

These treats were created equal for all foodie types to devour: vegan, g-free, vegetarian, and dairy-free lovers alike! I love rolling these finished bites in dark cocoa powder, crushed walnuts, or even matcha powder for a little extra flavor, creativity, and a pop of color. **Makes 12 to 15 date bars**

2 cups dried dates, pitted
¼ cup raw walnuts
¼ cup unsweetened shredded coconut
1 teaspoon organic vanilla extract

COATING
¼ cup unsweetened shredded coconut to top

In a food processor, pulse the pitted dates to create a thick paste. Add the walnuts, coconut, and vanilla and pulse until incorporated and a thick paste forms. Using a spatula, transfer the date mixture to a medium bowl.

Put the remaining ¼ cup unsweetened shredded coconut in a separate small, shallow bowl.

Working one at a time, using a spoon, scoop out about 2 tablespoons of the date mixture and, with clean hands, roll into a small rectangular 2- to 2½-inch x 1-inch bar. Coat the date bar with the coconut in the bowl, delicately pressing the shredded coconut onto the bar until lightly coated. Continue making bars with the remaining mixture.

Serve the bars in mini paper cupcake liners, or store in an airtight container for up to 1 week.

DARK CHOCOLATE–AVOCADO BROWNIES

These vegan brownies took at least thirty rounds of serious test-kitchen madness (not kidding!). When we finally said, okay, okay, moist *and* crumbly *and* chocolatey *and* delicious, we gave in. I used flaxseed meal and warm water to create a binder that replaces the need for egg. These egg-free, gluten-free, dairy-free, guilt-free brownies are some of the best you will ever taste! They will crumble a bit more than regular brownies, so beware of crumbs! **Makes 16 brownies**

Coconut oil or olive oil cooking spray, for the baking dish
Flaxseed egg: 1 tablespoon flaxseed meal,
    plus 3 tablespoons warm water
¾ cup gluten-free all-purpose flour
¾ cup unsweetened cocoa powder
1 teaspoon aluminum-free baking powder
½ teaspoon spirulina powder (optional)
¼ teaspoon sea salt
½ ripe avocado, pitted, peeled, and mashed until smooth
½ cup unrefined coconut oil
¼ cup hot water
1 teaspoon organic vanilla extract
½ cup packed organic light or dark brown sugar
1 teaspoon baking soda
1 tablespoon raw, unfiltered apple cider vinegar
1 cup semisweet or bittersweet chocolate chips
    (preferably with a minimum of 65 percent cacao) or
    1 cup chopped bittersweet chocolate (not milk or dairy chocolate)

Preheat the oven to 350°F. Lightly coat an 8- or 9-inch square baking dish with coconut oil spray and set aside (the smaller dish will yield slightly thicker brownies).

In a small bowl, combine the flaxseed meal and hot water; set aside to coagulate.

In a medium bowl, whisk together flour, cocoa powder, baking powder, spirulina, and salt. Set the dry ingredients aside.

In a large bowl, whisk together the avocado, water, coconut oil, and vanilla extract. Using an electric mixer, beat in the brown sugar to combine until the avocado is smooth. Add the dry ingredients to the wet, and beat well to combine.

In a small bowl, combine the baking soda and apple cider vinegar. When the mixture fizzes, use a spatula to stir into the brownie batter along with the coagulated flaxseeds. Gently fold in the chocolate chips. Scrape the batter into the prepared baking dish, and, using the spatula, smooth the surface.

Bake until the sides of the brownies are dry and pulling away from the pan and the center resists light pressure, 20 to 25 minutes.

Remove from the oven and set aside to cool for 1 hour. Then cut into 16 squares.

CLEAN GREEN TIP: I love to bake with avocados! Since not all avocados are created equal, you may not have a 100 percent smooth batter, and that's totally cool. If you can see some avocado pieces in the batter, don't worry about it. Once the brownies are baked (and you taste them), you won't even notice.

PUMPKIN MOCHI
TEA CAKE

The use of rice flour in this heavenly, aromatic, gluten-free tea cake makes it reminiscent of mochi, sweet desserts that are often used in Japanese cuisine. You can serve this cake sliced, or cut the loaf in half and create small squares for little snack cakes. This cake is the ultimate in tea-time socializing. **Yields one 8-inch loaf**

Coconut oil or olive oil cooking spray, for the loaf pan
3 large eggs, beaten
½ cup organic white sugar
⅓ cup unrefined coconut oil
2 tablespoons canned light coconut milk
½ cup canned 100 percent pure pumpkin purée
1 cup rice flour
½ teaspoon pumpkin pie spice
1 teaspoon aluminum-free baking powder

Preheat the oven to 350°F. Spray an 8 x 4-inch loaf pan with coconut oil or olive oil cooking spray.

In a large bowl, whisk together the eggs and sugar. Whisk in the unrefined coconut oil, coconut milk, and pumpkin purée. Slowly whisk in the rice flour, pumpkin pie spice, and baking powder.

When fully combined, pour the batter into the prepared loaf pan and bake for about 50 minutes, or until a toothpick inserted in the center comes out clean. Cool and slice into tiny bite-sized slices. Note that this recipe will not fill up the entire loaf pan; it makes a small loaf!

HOLIDAY SUGAR COOKIES

When I was about four years old, I first fell in love with cooking and baking during holiday season. I'll never forget making sugar cookies and gingerbread homes with my artistically talented mom and her super-creative friends, Cynthia in Sacramento and Rita in Bonsall, California. These incredible women taught me how much FUN cooking and baking can be and made a lasting impression on my heart for a lifetime. With half the butter out, and applesauce in, this "better-for-you" version of sugar cookies will make you and your kids smile, too. **Makes about 3 dozen cookies**

2¼ cups all-purpose flour (these work with gluten-free flour, as well)
1 teaspoon aluminum-free baking powder
½ teaspoon baking soda
½ teaspoon sea salt
½ cup organic granulated sugar
4 tablespoons (½ stick) unsalted butter, at room temperature
½ cup organic applesauce
1 large egg
1 teaspoon organic vanilla extract

ICING *(omit icing for a low-sugar cake and lightly dust with powdered sugar)*
2 cups confectioners' sugar
1 tablespoon unsalted butter, softened
1 teaspoon organic vanilla extract
1 to 2 tablespoons unsweetened almond milk (or as needed for desired consistency)

Preheat the oven to 350°F. Line several rimmed baking sheets with parchment paper. In a medium bowl, whisk together the flour, baking powder, baking soda, and salt. Set aside.

In the bowl of a stand mixer (or in a large bowl if using a hand mixer), cream the granulated sugar and butter together on medium speed until light and creamy, 1 to 1½ minutes. Add the applesauce, egg, and vanilla and beat to combine, using a rubber spatula to scrape down the sides and bottom of the bowl.

Turn the mixer off and add the reserved flour mixture. Beat on low speed just until combined, using a rubber spatula to scrape down the sides and bottom of the bowl as needed. Cover the bowl with plastic wrap and place in the refrigerator. Chill the cookie dough for at least 25 to 30 minutes, or overnight for best results.

On a clean, floured work surface, roll out the chilled dough to a thickness of ¼ inch. Cut the dough with floured cookie cutters. Place the cookies about 1 inch apart on the lined baking sheets. Bake until no indentation remains when touched, 10 to 12 minutes. Let the cookies cool on the baking sheets for 10 minutes, then transfer them to wire racks to cool completely.

While the cookies are cooling, make the icing. In a medium bowl (or in the bowl of a stand mixer), whisk together the confectioners' sugar, softened butter, vanilla, and almond milk until well combined.

Decorate the cookies as desired. Make sure to cool your sugar cookies completely prior to icing! Heat will melt your icing right off of the cookies.

VEGAN DARK CHOCOLATE–AVOCADO CAKE

This decadent, fudgy, and dense cake quickly became "the favorite" out of all my vegan baking recipes. Perhaps it's the use of cocoa powder or delicious, creamy, and good-for-you avocados and coconut oil. Whatever the reasons (probably the chemical endorphins that are released after eating chocolate!), we all went mad for it. If you're making this cake for a special occasion, you can double the recipe and make a two-layer cake. **Serves 12; makes one 8- or 9-inch round cake**

Coconut oil or olive oil cooking spray, for the cake pan
1¾ cups gluten-free flour (look for Bob's Red Mill brand)
1 cup almond meal
¾ cup unsweetened cocoa powder
1 teaspoon aluminum-free baking powder
¼ teaspoon salt
1 ripe avocado, pitted, peeled, and mashed until smooth
½ cup organic granulated sugar
1½ cups water
⅓ cup unrefined coconut oil, melted
1 teaspoon organic vanilla extract
1 tablespoon raw, unfiltered apple cider vinegar
1 teaspoon baking soda

ICING *(if making a low-sugar cake, omit icing and lightly dust with cocoa powder)*
5 cups confectioners' sugar
2 to 4 teaspoons almond or coconut milk
½ cup chocolate-hazelnut butter
¼ cup unsweetened cocoa powder

Preheat the oven to 350°F. Cut a round parchment paper base for the bottom of the cake pan(s). Grease an 8-inch cake pan with coconut oil or olive oil spray, place the parchment paper round inside, and set aside.

In a large bowl, whisk together the flour, almond meal, cocoa powder, baking powder, and salt.

In a separate large bowl, combine the fully mashed avocado and granulated sugar. Slowly stir in the water, coconut oil, and vanilla extract.

Slowly incorporate the flour mixture into the wet ingredients, stirring until the avocado is completely smooth. In a small bowl or measuring cup, combine the baking soda and apple cider vinegar and let them fizz. Add to the final cake batter. Batter will be thick.

Pour the cake batter into the prepared cake pan, and bake on the middle rack for 20 minutes, or until a toothpick inserted in the center comes out clean. Let the cake cool in the pan, then transfer to a plate or cake stand.

While the cake is baking, make the icing. Using a stand mixer or hand mixer, beat together the confectioners' sugar, chocolate-hazelnut butter, and cocoa powder until smooth. Slowly add the almond milk and continue beating until combined.

When the cake is completely cool, spread the icing evenly across the top and sides using an offset spatula.

When baking with cocoa, remember this smart tip: Baking powder helps to retain flavanols otherwise lost in baking. See page 243 for a Clean Green Tip on avocados.

BANANA CHOCOLATE CHIP COOKIE DOUGH "ICE CREAM"

Be sure to peel your ripe bananas and freeze them in a resealable freezer bag the night before making this delish faux "ice cream." Enjoy with some extra chocolate or carob chips and a sprinkle of coconut shavings on top. **Yields about 2 cups**

3 ripe, frozen bananas, peeled
½ cup almond meal
¼ cup almond and coconut milk blend
1 teaspoon ground cinnamon
2 teaspoons organic vanilla extract

TOPPING
¼ cup mini chocolate chips or ¼ cup dark dairy-free chocolate, chopped
   (use carob chips if vegan or dairy-free)

Combine the ingredients for ice cream in a blender (preferably a Vitamix) and blend until smooth. Use the Vitamix tamper stick to whip up all the bananas until fully combined and creamy. You are looking for an extra-thick smoothie or soft-serve consistency. Sprinkle in chocolate chips and fold in with a spatula. Serve immediately. For a firmer texture, double the batch and pour into an 8-inch loaf tin, cover, and freeze until ready to serve! This cookie dough faux ice cream keeps for up to 1 week in an airtight container in the freezer.

GREEN MATCHA TEA
LOAF CAKE

With matcha tea and coffee everywhere, I wanted to come up with a simple one-loaf-pan recipe that everyone could enjoy with their daily cup. Inspired by Mom, and all of her tea parties and company over while I was growing up, this has become my go-to loaf when I'm having friends over for coffee or tea. It also makes a lovely hostess gift! **Yields one 8-inch loaf**

Coconut oil or olive oil cooking spray, to coat the loaf pan

DRY INGREDIENTS

1¾ cups all-purpose or gluten-free flour

2 tablespoons high-quality matcha tea powder, plus 2 teaspoons

1 teaspoon aluminum-free baking powder

1 teaspoon baking soda

¼ teaspoon sea salt

WET INGREDIENTS

4 tablespoons (½ stick) unsalted butter, softened

1 ripe banana, peeled and mashed

⅓ cup organic sugar

1 teaspoon organic vanilla extract

2 large eggs

½ cup plus 2 tablespoons unsweetened almond milk

Preheat the oven to 350°F. Lightly coat a 8 x 4-inch loaf pan with coconut oil or olive oil cooking spray.

In a medium bowl, whisk together the flour, matcha tea powder, baking powder, baking soda, and salt and set aside.

In a large bowl, using a whisk, blend the butter and banana to combine. Add the sugar and beat until fluffy. Add the vanilla extract and the eggs, one at a time, scraping down the sides of the bowl as needed.

Slowly mix in the dry ingredients, alternating with the almond milk, until well combined. Pour the batter into the prepared loaf pan and bake for 35 to 40 minutes. Remove from the oven when the top has cracked a bit and the loaf is firm to the touch and let it cool. Enjoy with a cup of joe with homemade almond milk or green roasted brown rice tea!

CHOCOLATE CHIP
PUMPKIN LOAF

Chocolate plus pumpkin: simple, moist, delicious. Enough said.

Yields one 8-inch loaf

Coconut oil or olive oil cooking spray, for the loaf pan

3 tablespoons unsalted butter, softened

½ cup packed organic dark or light brown sugar

2 large eggs

1¾ cups (one 15-ounce can) 100 percent pure pumpkin purée

2 tablespoons unsweetened almond milk

1¾ cups all-purpose or gluten-free flour

1 teaspoon baking soda

1 teaspoon aluminum-free baking powder

2 teaspoons pumpkin pie spice

¼ teaspoon sea salt

1 cup semisweet chocolate chips or mini-semisweet chocolate chips

Preheat the oven to 350°F. Line an 8 x 4-inch loaf pan with parchment paper and lightly coat with coconut oil or olive oil cooking spray.

In a large bowl, using a whisk, gently combine the softened butter with brown sugar and add the eggs, one at a time. Add the puréed pumpkin and the unsweetened almond milk and whisk to combine. Set aside the wet ingredients.

In a separate medium bowl, combine the flour, baking soda, baking powder, pumpkin pie spice, and sea salt. Using a rubber spatula, fold the dry ingredients into the wet, then gently fold in the chocolate chips.

Bake the bread on the middle rack for about 40 minutes, or until the top is golden brown and the loaf is firm to the touch. Allow the loaf to cool before handling.

When the bread is cool, slice with a serrated knife. Spread with a dollop of pumpkin butter or regular butter for an extra-special treat.

MATCHA-PISTACHIO-CHOCOLATE TRUFFLES

With decadent dark chocolate, rich and earthy matcha powder, and heart-healthy pistachios, this is the perfect dessert for anyone looking for a feel-good-antioxidant boost. Pack these truffles for a little midday pick-me-up when you're craving something sweet! **Makes about 3 dozen truffles**

3 cups premium dark chocolate chips (look for dairy-free, minimum 60 percent cacao)
½ cup heavy cream, at room temperature
⅓ cup pistachios, shelled and pulsed in a food processor to a fine meal
1 tablespoon matcha powder, plus 1 teaspoon for dusting

Line a pan with parchment paper. In a large saucepan, bring 2 to 3 cups of water to a simmer. Create a warm water bath by placing a heatproof glass or stainless-steel bowl over the saucepan of simmering water. Add the chocolate chips and heavy cream to the bowl. Mix well with a spatula to combine as the chocolate melts.

Remove the bowl from the heat and transfer the chocolate mixture to a parchment paper–lined loaf pan or shallow bowl and cool completely to room temperature. Place into the fridge for 90 minutes to solidify.

Using a small melon baller, scoop out the truffle mixture and mold into 1-inch balls. If you don't have a melon baller, use your hands.

Fill a small bowl with the crushed pistachios, roll the truffles in the pistachios, pressing the nuts gently into the surface. Using a fine-mesh strainer or sifter, dust the truffles with the matcha powder.

Transfer the truffles to paper cupcake liners or a parchment paper–lined tin and refrigerate until ready to serve. I like to keep mine in my favorite tin—thanks, Dean!

CLEAN GREEN TIP: Cocoa is one of the richest sources of flavanols, which are plant compounds that help protect the heart. The more flavanols, the higher the percentage of cocoa and the more bitter the chocolate. Look for at least 60 percent cocoa content when purchasing cocoa or chocolate.

HOMEMADE
COCONUT CAKE

This delicious "funfetti" cake is a fabulously updated and better-for-you version of the '80s birthday party staple, made with ripe bananas, almond meal, and coconut oil. This is the last recipe I developed for this book, and it was the last recipe to be shot . . . and it turned out to be just about everyone's favorite. Perhaps because it was the "wrap/final" recipe, perhaps because it is so beautiful. Whatever the reason, this cake represents what a dessert is supposed to be—fun! Double it if making a layer cake for a special celebration. **Serves 12; makes one 8- or 9-inch round cake**

Coconut oil or olive oil cooking spray, for the cake pan

WET INGREDIENTS

⅓ cup unrefined coconut oil, at room temperature

⅓ cup organic white sugar

1 ripe banana, peeled and mashed

¾ cup water

1 teaspoon organic vanilla extract

DRY INGREDIENTS

2 cups gluten-free flour

¾ cup almond meal

1 teaspoon aluminum-free baking powder

¼ teaspoon sea salt

1 teaspoon baking soda

1 tablespoon unfiltered apple cider vinegar

2 tablespoons multicolored rainbow sprinkles*

COCONUT ICING *(omit icing for a low-sugar cake and lightly dust with powdered sugar)*

2 ½–3 cups cups confectioners' sugar

2 tablespoons unrefined coconut oil

* Read ingredients on the label carefully if you are strictly vegan/dairy-free/gluten-free. "Let's Do . . . Organic Sprinklz" is a sprinkle brand that is organic, gluten-free, and vegan!

3 tablespoons unsweetened almond milk

1 teaspoon apple cider vinegar

2 tablespoons multicolored rainbow sprinkles (see organic brand note on page 259)

Preheat the oven to 350°F. Lightly coat a 8- or 9-inch round cake pan with unrefined coconut oil or olive oil baking spray.

In a medium bowl, whisk together the unrefined coconut oil, granulated sugar, banana, water, and vanilla extract; set the wet ingredients aside.

In a small bowl, mix together the gluten-free flour, almond meal, baking powder, and salt. Gently add the dry ingredients to the wet ingredients in the medium bowl and mix until combined; do not overmix.

In a small bowl, combine the baking soda and apple cider vinegar mixture, allow the mixture to fizz, and fold into the cake batter. Batter will be thick. Gently fold in the sprinkles just before baking.

Pour the batter into the prepared cake pan, and bake in the preheated oven for about 26 to 30 minutes (every oven is different, so be sure to test doneness with a toothpick), or until the top is golden brown.

Remove the cake from the oven and cool completely before icing.

While the cake is cooling, in a large bowl with a handheld mixer (or in the bowl of a stand mixer with whisk attachment), add the confectioners' sugar, unrefined coconut oil, and almond milk and whisk to combine. Beat in the apple cider vinegar. Make sure icing is stiff.

Gently place the cooled cake on a cake stand or a pretty serving plate. Using a spatula, ice the top, then the sides, and finish with rainbow sprinkles before the frosting hardens! Enjoy the cake with a bottle of Champagne, some fabulous friends, and good music. It's magic!

14

CLEAN GREEN
BASICS

SIMPLICITY IS THE ULTIMATE
SOPHISTICATION.
—Leonardo da Vinci

HOMEMADE
ALMOND MILK

If you love unsweetened almond milk, you will love this decadent and creamy way to make almond milk at home. I love finishing mine off with a touch of maple syrup, honey, and even some cinnamon or nutmeg. Try out this recipe and use it to top off Amaranth Berry Porridge (page 94) or pour a little bit over my Cinnamon-Spiced Granola (page 80). Simple and with no additives, preservatives, or processing! **Yields 5 cups**

3 cups raw almonds
4 to 5 cups water (for soaking)
5 cups purified water

EQUIPMENT
Cheesecloth, string, or rubber band, blender, bowl

In a large mixing bowl, submerge 3 cups raw almonds in water overnight or for up to 8 hours. Strain the almonds and discard the water.

In a high-powered blender, blend the almonds carefully with 5 cups purified water to combine well.

Tie a 12 x 12-inch square of cheesecloth with a rubber band or string over a large mixing bowl and gently pour the almond blend into the cheesecloth to strain all the liquid out.

Reserve the liquid, add a touch of cinnamon or pumpkin pie spice, and enjoy! Yields approximately 5 cups of delish, homemade, and extra-creamy almond milk. Store for approximately 5 days in a glass container in the fridge.

HOMEMADE ALMOND BUTTER

Homemade nut butters are so simple to whip up yourself, and you can make large batches as long as you store them in the fridge. With no preservatives, sweeteners, or additives, this simple toss-and-pulse recipe will make you a believer. Plus it is *so* much more delicious than the store-bought stuff! Once you start making nut butter at home, I promise, you will cross it off of your grocery list once and for all.

Yields 5 cups

3 cups raw almonds

Place the almonds into a food processor or high-powered blender and pulse until completely smooth and creamy. (Turn off and use a spatula to scrape down the sides if needed.)

You can add a touch of coconut oil, almond oil, or sea salt if desired.

HOMEMADE CURRY KETCHUP

Love curry powder and all of its magnificent anti-inflammatory benefits? With the addition of lycopene plus vitamin C from the tomatoes, you'll devour this smarter homemade ketchup—a delicious and effortless way to spice up your fries, burgers, lentil loaf, and more. **Yields about 16 ounces**

2 tablespoons extra-virgin olive oil
1 yellow onion, finely diced
2 tablespoons curry powder
1 teaspoon granulated garlic powder
2 tablespoons tomato paste
One 28-ounce can organic crushed tomatoes
¼ cup apple cider vinegar
2 tablespoons packed organic brown sugar
½ teaspoon salt

In a large pot over medium-low heat, combine the olive oil, onion, curry powder, and garlic powder and cook until the onion is soft and spices are fragrant, about 8 minutes.

Add the tomato paste, diced tomatoes, apple cider vinegar, brown sugar, and salt. Simmer, uncovered, over medium-low heat for about 1 hour, or until thickened.

Remove the pot from heat and let the mixture cool slightly. Transfer to a food processor or blender and blend until smooth. Serve up with those sweet potato fries or store in the fridge in an airtight container for up to 2 weeks.

HOMEMADE KALE MARINARA SAUCE

I developed this delicious homemade marinara recipe with vitamins, minerals, and the powerful antioxidant lycopene in mind. With each and every ingredient packed with health benefits, this sauce will become a household staple. Make a large batch and freeze whatever you're not using immediately so you always have it on hand—it will keep in the freezer for up to six months! Just thaw as needed.

Yields 4 cups

2 tablespoons extra-virgin olive oil
1 yellow onion, finely chopped
4 garlic cloves, finely minced
Two 28-ounce cans unsalted organic crushed or diced tomatoes
¼ cup fresh oregano leaves
¼ teaspoon sea salt
2 tablespoons balsamic vinegar
1 cup finely julienned lacinato kale leaves

In a large stockpot, warm the extra-virgin olive oil over low heat. Add the diced onion and cook for about 10 minutes, or until soft. Add the garlic and sauté for another 3 minutes on low heat.

Add the crushed tomatoes and fresh oregano leaves and give the sauce a good stir. Cook on low for about 2 hours, stirring occasionally to prevent burning.

When the sauce has reduced and thickened, finish with the sea salt, balsamic vinegar, and julienned kale. Simmer for an additional 5 minutes and serve or use in recipes as needed.

CLEAN GREEN TIP: Canned tomatoes actually contain higher amounts of the antioxidant lycopene than fresh tomatoes. And your body absorbs the nutrients in canned tomatoes better than fresh. Sounds crazy, but it's totally true. Tomatoes are heated before they're canned, and this temperature change makes lycopene easier for the body to absorb. So store those canned tomatoes as a household staple!

HOMEMADE APPLE CIDER QUICK PICKLES

These simple and quick apple cider vinegar pickles are the perfect balance of acidity and add a little crunch to your clean green burgers and sandwiches. They also hold beautifully in a mason jar in your fridge for up to 3 months! **Yields approximately 2 cups**

2 cucumbers, cut into thin ⅛- to ¼-inch slices on a mandoline
1½ teaspoons sea salt
2 cups raw, unfiltered apple cider vinegar
½ cup packed organic brown sugar
½ yellow onion, thinly sliced on a mandoline
1 teaspoon caraway seeds
1 teaspoon fennel seeds

Place the cucumber slices in a colander and set in the sink. Sprinkle with the salt and toss to coat. Let stand for 20 minutes. Rinse, drain, and transfer the cucumbers to a large heatproof bowl.

Meanwhile, combine the apple cider vinegar, brown sugar, onion, caraway seeds, and fennel seeds in a medium saucepan and bring to a boil. Reduce the heat and let mixture simmer for 10 minutes. Pour the hot liquid over the bowl of cucumbers and stir to combine. Cool to room temperature, refrigerate.

15

TEN CLEAN GREEN SALAD DRESSINGS

Welcome to the world of clean green salad dressings. You can whip up virtually hundreds of different dressings at home—all you need is an arsenal of recipes. Here's my gift to you: ten creatively delicious, low-sugar, nutrient-packed dressings to get your greens all dressed up without any processed chemicals, additives, excess sugars, or preservatives.

CARROT-GINGER VINAIGRETTE

If you love the subtle sweetness of carrots balanced with the acidity of rice vinegar, the spice from ginger, and the saltiness of tamari, you're gonna die when you taste this delicious, oil-free dressing—perfect over a bowl of mixed greens and brown rice. **Yields 1¼ cups**

3 carrots, peeled and roughly chopped
2 tablespoons yellow onion, roughly chopped
½ cup rice vinegar
2 tablespoons reduced-sodium tamari soy sauce
2 tablespoons water
2 tablespoons peeled and roughly chopped fresh ginger

Combine all of the ingredients in a blender and blend until smooth. Store the dressing in a resealable glass jar, refrigerated, for up to 2 weeks.

CLEAN GREEN TIP: Dressing should never drown your greens! When you make your own clean, simple dressings, the flavor will pack such a punch that a little will go a long way.

CREAMY MISO DRESSING

Miso, a fermented soybean paste the Japanese have been cooking with for centuries, is full of natural manganese, copper, zinc, and vitamin K. It's also packed with tummy-friendly bacteria and cancer-fighting antioxidants. As my mom always says, " . . . tastes YUM!" **Yields 1 cup**

6 tablespoons olive oil mayonnaise
3 tablespoons miso paste (preferably red)
6 tablespoons rice vinegar
1 teaspoon ginger powder

In a small bowl, whisk together all the ingredients until well combined. Store the dressing in a resealable glass jar, in the fridge, for up to 2 weeks.

SKINNY CAESAR DRESSING

With the Greek yogurt, balsamic vinegar, Dijon mustard, roasted garlic, and lemon juice, this healthy version of the traditionally calorie-packed Caesar dressing adds indulgent creaminess and a bright burst of flavor to any fresh greens or grains. **Yields ⅔ cup**

⅓ cup Greek yogurt
2 tablespoons extra-virgin olive oil
1 tablespoons Dijon mustard
1 tablespoon balsamic vinegar
1 tablespoon Worcestershire sauce (optional)
1 teaspoon fresh lemon juice
2 roasted garlic cloves, crushed
¼ teaspoon freshly ground black pepper

In a small bowl, whisk together all the ingredients until well combined. Store the dressing in a resealable glass jar, in the fridge, for up to 2 weeks.

CLEAN GREEN GODDESS DRESSING

This delicious, vibrant green dressing is a perfect option for serving with a platter of crudités, spreading on a wrap or sandwich, and even topping a juicy burger.

Yields 1 cup

½ large avocado, pitted, peeled, and halved
2 scallions finely chopped
¼ cup fresh parsley leaves
½ cup Greek yogurt
2 tablespoons olive oil mayonnaise
1 tablespoon Worcestershire sauce (optional)
2 tablespoons fresh lemon juice
¼ teaspoon sea salt (optional)

Combine all the ingredients in a blender and blend on high. Store the dressing in a resealable glass jar, in the fridge, for up to 2 weeks.

APPLE CIDER VINAIGRETTE

Unfiltered apple cider vinegar is so good for you in so many ways—from stimulating your circulation to clearing up breakouts. It is also adds a slightly sweet tang to any dressing. I love it paired with a bit of mustard and honey— delish. **Yields 3½ ounces**

¼ cup unfiltered apple cider vinegar
2 tablespoons extra-virgin olive oil
¼ teaspoon sea salt
1 tablespoon Dijon mustard
1 teaspoon manuka honey or maple syrup

In a small bowl, whisk together all the ingredients until well combined. Store the dressing in a resealable glass jar, in the fridge, for up to 2 weeks.

SOY-LIME VINAIGRETTE

This delicious combination of lime plus soy is as cleansing to the body as it is refreshing to the palate. I love using this delicious dressing for a marinade for chicken, fish, or tofu. **Yields 3½ ounces**

2 tablespoons extra-virgin olive oil
2 tablespoons reduced-sodium tamari soy sauce
3 tablespoons fresh lime juice
1 tablespoon balsamic vinaigrette

In a small bowl, whisk together all the ingredients until well combined. Store the dressing in a resealable glass jar, in the fridge, for up to 2 weeks.

CLEAN GREEN LEMON
VINAIGRETTE

You know by now how much I love lemons and believe in their cleansing and antioxidant powers. The fresh lemon juice and honey in this recipe offer the perfect balance of sweet and tart, and a little zing from the Dijon pulls it all together. This is your go-to, anytime recipe for dressing greens and grains—simple and delicious. **Yields ½ cup**

¼ cup fresh lemon juice
2 tablespoons extra-virgin olive oil
1 tablespoon Dijon mustard
1 teaspoon honey or maple syrup
¹/₁₆ teaspoon sea salt

In a medium bowl, whisk together all the ingredients until well combined. Store the dressing in a resealable glass jar, in fridge, for up to 1 week.

RED WINE–HONEY
MUSTARD

Dijon is my favorite binding agent in homemade dressings, with the addition of red wine vinegar and honey, this simple recipe brightens up any bowl. **Yields ⅓ cup**

2 tablespoons red wine vinegar
1 tablespoon Dijon mustard
1 teaspoon honey or maple syrup
2 tablespoons extra-virgin olive oil

In a small bowl, whisk together all the ingredients until well combined. Store the dressing in a resealable glass jar, in the fridge, for up to 1 week.

LIGHT BARBECUE RANCH DRESSING

My mother always whips up the best homemade ranch dressing, and I finally got her to send me the recipe. In the meantime, this BBQ ranch, made with just five ingredients, should do the trick. **Yields ½ cup**

¼ cup store-bought or homemade barbecue sauce
¼ cup Greek yogurt
1 tablespoon unfiltered, raw apple cider vinegar
1 teaspoon dried oregano
¼ teaspoon sea salt

In a small bowl, whisk together all the ingredients until well combined. Store the dressing in a resealable glass jar, in the fridge, for up to 1 week*.

* Make sure to read the label if buying jarred BBQ sauce—some brands contain gluten, though most don't. Also, look for a sauce that is lower in sugar and sodium—some brands contain sky-high amounts of both!

COCONUT-LIME DRESSING

Coconut plus lime. It doesn't get any better than that. Put the lime in the coconut . . . and enjoy. **Yields ½ cup**

¼ cup canned light coconut milk

2 tablespoons fresh lime juice

2 tablespoons Vegenaise or olive oil mayonnaise

¼ teaspoon sweet paprika

⅛ teaspoon sea salt

¼ teaspoon peeled and grated fresh ginger

In a small bowl, whisk together all the ingredients until well combined. Store the dressing in a resealable glass jar, in the fridge, for up to 1 week.

CLEAN GREEN TIP: Light coconut milk is one of the best ingredients for achieving a rich and flavorful consistency in curry dishes, soups, marinades, and, of course, dressings. Be mindful to use it in moderation, as it's high in fat and calories—and whenever possible, opt for light coconut milk. Light coconut milk comes from the second press of coconut milk, while regular comes from the first.

ACKNOWLEDGMENTS

My utmost thanks and grace for so many of you who allowed me to dream in color and simply shine; this book is for all of you:

Mom, the most wonderful and incredible woman on this planet. You are the strongest woman I know, the most graceful, the most kind, the most talented. I admire you, your life, and your heart. To be half as good as you, I would be so lucky. Thank you for being my heart!

Dad, this year has been a year of wonder for you! You are shining and smiling more than ever! I am so lucky to have been raised with your incredible work ethic, big heart, and gracious soul. Thank you for being a wonderful father and husband to Mom.

Jenni, for all the ways you teach me to be green, I'm amazed. You're always ahead of the game, doing what is right, not because it's popular, but because it is the right thing to do. I admire you and your dedication to your craft.

For Dean, you have forever made an imprint on my heart. When you came into my life, you made me forget about the world, you showed me how to just be me. Thank you for being an incredible friend, for holding my hand and my heart. My love grows with you every day and I am so grateful for your big heart, your big smile, and your nonstop enthusiasm for life. I love you.

For Karen Rinaldi and Julie Will at Harper Wave: thank you, ladies, for giving me opportunity. For allowing me to be me and for embracing my femininity, for celebrating my work. You are both incredibly talented, you are both such a pleasure to work with, and are unreal at what you do. I am grateful for your human touch. Congrats on the incredible success of Harper Wave; I am honored to

work with you both. Julie, you are the best editor I have been able to work with thus far, and I am so grateful to learn from the best.

For Eric Lupfer, my literary agent at WME: for all of the incredible hard work you put toward this project and the support you give your clients, thank you! I am grateful for your time, efforts, and mentorship throughout this process.

Sydney Pierce, Leigh Raynor, and Penny Makras: thank you for the book support, the love, and the incredible hard work. Your support and hands to hold through this process have been immeasurable!

For Evi Abeler! For such beautiful and treasured photography and, more important, the strength to get through such a large-scale project, together. Thank you, Evi, and to Mary Rinfret, your lovely agent!

Farmer Lee Jones, Mary Jones, Bob and Aaron Jones, and to the dedicated team at the Chef's Garden! Chef Jamie, Chef Ülfet, and Andrew! To an incredible shoot at the farm, for making us feel right at home. And to all of your hardworking staff-farmers, we are grateful beyond words for the incredible hospitality.

For the awesome shoot team! Jade Rosenberg and Cecilia Busick, for your incredible hard work, organization, dedication, and love! For Molly Shuster, Drew Salvatore, Rebecca Bartoshesky, thank you for the beautiful food and prop styling. Rebecca S., Jordan, Jenny, and Cecelia S., thank you for the time on set and all of your contributions! For Danielle Zaria, my darling publicist, thank you!

For the fabulous food stylists: Laurie Knoop, Tyler Hill, Kathleen Morton, thank you for your *amazing support* and for being so enthusiastic to work with!

The fabulous Culinary Vegetable Institute team! Anna Christoff, Alex, Jessica: thank you for your hospitality and your grace! You made us feel right at home.

Kristen Arnett, you have been such an incredible friend to my heart and soul in NYC; thank you. I cherish our time together, friends and sisters.

For Karen Kreutner, thank you for all of the love and delicious recipes you have shared with me. My heart is so grateful for your love and kindness. ;)

For my girls in Cali! Stephanie, Christina, Andy, Tina, Suzanne, Case, Courts, Michelle, and Chrystal—and Danie in Hawaii! Thank you, ladies—for being here for me, for listening, for your advice, and for all of your guidance, forever, I am grateful.

For my family, Aunt Takuko and Baachan, for sharing our Japanese culture with my heart. For the Kumai and Gwiazdowski families, this book is for all of you.

For my agents at WME: My love and heart are always so grateful: Justin

Ongert, Strand Conover, Jeff Googel, Amir Shahkhalili, Dave Sherman, Rob Koslowski, Bethany Dick, and Jenni Levine. Thank you for your loyal efforts and love, my heart is full. For Rachel Gorman, Halle Mureck: you ladies help me to smile every week; thank you for your hard work and sunshine love.

For my sweet Rona Tison and Rushmi Soni at Ito En, for the incredible Cassidy at Bob's Red Mill, Linda at Almond Breeze, Frances and Brandy at Hurom, and Allison at Vitamix.

For Shari Gab at ABC Home, we are always so grateful! For Aloft Studios NYC, Kim and John, for always being my family! For MTC Kitchen and the amazing Japanese props, *domo arigato*!

For my family at the E! Networks and my NBC family. For Dr. Mehmet Oz and your team and Food Network, CosmoBody, Cosmo, and Rodale, thank you for continuing to share my very best work. I am truly grateful for the opportunities you bring.

For all my girlfriends who keep my ass busy and fit, I love you NY girls: Amy, Jonette, and Julie (at Bar Method!). My NYC gals Molly, Jenelle, Adrianna, and Sajel!

For the glam squad galore in 2014: Robert, Mai, Juli, Janis, Flynn, Henry, Glo, thank you all for being the most fab glam squad and for always keepin' it real.

For Kenshiro at Sun Noodles, the Wedderspoon honey ladies Briana and Kelly! For Marukome, Justin's Nut Butter, Genesis Today, Nutrex Hawaii, Boxed Water, and the Chia Seed Co, thank you for all of your generosity!

For you, the reader, my heart sends its utmost love and thanks, for I am forever grateful for your heart, for your kindness, and for allowing me to share my love of good food with you. For God/the Universe for watching over me and my heart, thank you. I promise to forever keep it real yo. Xx Candice.

INDEX

Page references in *italics* refer to illustrations.

ABOUT THE AUTHOR

Candice Kumai is a four-time bestselling author, chef, and health journalist. As *E! News'* resident food and health expert, she is the cohost of the food special *Food Envy*. She is the former host of Lifetime's *Cook Yourself Thin* and TLC's *Homemade Simple*.

At age twenty-three, Candice Kumai was the youngest chef to compete on Bravo's inaugural season of *Top Chef*. After almost a decade of fashion modeling, and a degree in interpersonal communications, she received her professional training from Le Cordon Bleu College of Culinary Arts in California, and she has written and developed recipes for more than half a dozen cookbooks, including *The Skinny Bitch Cookbook*, *Recipe Rehab*, *Novak Djokovic's Serve to Win*, and *The Bikini Body Diet*.

Candice has been featured regularly on *Access Hollywood*, *Dr. Oz*, *The Today Show*, *CBS Early Show*, *GMA*, *The Doctors*, *The Talk*, *Extra*, the Cooking Channel, the Food Network, *Top Chef*, *Iron Chef*, *Simply Ming*, and *Beat Bobby Flay*.

She is the former food editor at large at *Shape* and *Men's Fitness*, and her previous cookbooks include *Cook Yourself Thin*, *Pretty Delicious*, *Cook Yourself Sexy*, and *Clean Green Drinks*. Candice is featured in and contribut to dozens of food, health, beauty, fashion, and lifestyle publications. lends her efforts to dozens of food-, culture-, and wellness- based non organizations. She resides in New York City.